PRAISE FOR THE DARK NOVELS

'A wholly engrossing and sophisticated spy novel set against a forgotten corner of 20th century history. Fascinating and compelling' – William Boyd, author of *Solo*

'A cross between James Bond and Jason Bourne... carefully researched so the history is credible, even instructive... The action is fast and violent and so is the hero' – *Literary Review*

'A taut and tortured exploration of betrayal on the national, ideological and personal levels simultaneously... A cleverly twisted tale of intrigue and deception, this is a masterly excursion back to the bad old days of the Cold War' – *The Times*

'The immediacy of Duns' writing grabs and suspends the reader in a beautifully realized heartbeat of recent history' – *Kirkus Reviews*

PRAISE FOR *DEAD DROP*

'This excellent book contains lessons that are still valid in the 21st century' – Oleg Gordievsky in *Literary Review*

'Startling and convincing...an irresistible real-life thriller' – Francis Wheen in *The Mail on Sunday*

Jeremy Duns was born in 1973 and was educated at St Catherine's College, Oxford. He is the author of the Paul Dark series of spy novels and *Dead Drop*, a non-fiction book about Oleg Penkovsky. He lives with his family in the Åland archipelago.

Duns on Bond

An Omnibus of Journalism on Ian Fleming and James Bond

JEREMY DUNS

SKERRY

DUNS ON BOND

ALSO BY JEREMY DUNS

Free Agent
Song of Treason
The Moscow Option
The Dark Chronicles (omnibus)
Spy Out The Land
Dead Drop (Codename: Hero in the US)

Shorts
News of Devils
Cabal
Tradecraft
Agent Of Influence

DUNS ON BOND

This edition first published March 20 2016. The right of Jeremy Duns to be identified as the Author of this work has been asserted in accordance with the Copyright, Designs and Patents Act 1988.

Cover photograph: Christopher Burns, Unsplash
Design: JJD Productions/Skerry

All rights reserved. No part of this book may be reprinted or reproduced or utilised in any form or by any electronic, mechanical, or other means, now known or hereafter invented, including photocopying and recording, or in any information storage or retrieval system, without permission in writing from the publishers.

Contents

Introduction

Diamonds in The Rough

    1. Gold Dust
    2. Uncut Gem
    3. Commando Bond
    4. Black Tie Spy
    5. SMERSH vs SMERSH
    6. Bourne Yesterday

Rogue Royale

    Notes for *Rogue Royale*

    From the author
    Acknowledgements

Introduction

THIS BOOK IS an omnibus edition of two short books: *Diamonds In The Rough* and *Rogue Royale*. *Diamonds in The Rough* is a collection of six articles about the cinematic and literary worlds of Ian Fleming and James Bond. Both have, of course, already been covered in scores of other books, articles and documentaries, and one would be forgiven for thinking there's no ground left to cover. But in the last few years, I've investigated some lesser-known, and in some cases completely unknown, facets of Ian Fleming's world, and I hope found a few diamonds lurking in the rough. Some of the material in this book has previously been published in newspapers, magazines and online, but all of it has been revised and in some cases greatly expanded.

The opening article, *Gold Dust,* is about my hunt for *Per Fine Ounce*, the lost James Bond novel by South African thriller-writer Geoffrey Jenkins. This first appeared in issue 2 of *Kiss Kiss Bang Bang* magazine back in 2005, and I've made just a few revisions. The full draft of the book has sadly still not been found, but Jenkins' estate published a novel with the same title by Peter Vollmer in September 2014 as a result of this story, inspired by the surviving material.

Uncut Gem builds on research I published in *The Sunday Times* in 2010, examining the attempts to film Ian Fleming's non-fiction book *The Diamond Smugglers*. I've gone into a lot more detail here than in previously published versions, about the background of the book, the contents of the screenplay I unearthed, and the prolonged efforts to turn the property into a serious rival to the Bond films. John Collard's family very kindly gave me access to a huge amount of material, including private correspondence, IDSO agents' reports, and the complete manuscript of Collard's book.

In *Commando Bond*, I look at how Ian Fleming incorporated elements of real life into his novels, and explore the numerous references and allusions to special forces. Fleming's use of real operations had a curious cinematic echo after his death, as I explore in *Black Tie Spy*, an extension of an article I originally submitted to *The Sunday Telegraph*. The seed for my research here was planted when I was writing a novel. I'd plotted out a chapter set during the Second World War in which my protagonist, a British secret agent, is sent on a mission to an island in the Baltic. But as I came to write it, I realized I was unsure how he should reach the island. Would he have been sent by parachute? By submarine? Or some other way? I reached for one of my most thumbed books, M.R.D. Foot's official history of the Special Operations Executive, to refresh my memory on how that organization had inserted secret agents behind enemy lines during the war. To my surprise, I found myself reading a passage I hadn't paid sufficient notice to before, which mentioned an operation undertaken by MI6 in 1941. Those few lines took me on a fascinating journey into the origins of one of the best loved moments in modern cinema: the opening scene of *Goldfinger*.

For *SMERSH vs SMERSH*, I hop over to the other side of the Iron Curtain to compare the real organization of that name with the one Fleming created for his novels, tracing his research into Soviet intelligence. Who inspired Rosa Klebb and Red Grant? This is where you'll find out.

Bourne Yesterday, first published on my website, looks at Ian Fleming's influence on the Jason Bourne series, and the influences on his own work. After this comes *Rogue Royale*, in which I investigate Ben Hecht's screenplays for *Casino Royale*.

So please, grab your wetsuit and Champion harpoon gun and join me as I dive in to the world of Ian Fleming and James Bond.

Jeremy Duns
Mariehamn, December 2014

Diamonds in the Rough

Investigations into the Worlds of Ian Fleming and James Bond

JEREMY DUNS

For Johanna, with love

Gold Dust

SINCE IAN FLEMING'S DEATH, a few snippets of information have cropped up that have both fascinated and frustrated Bond fans. One of these is the 'lost novel' *Per Fine Ounce*. A James Bond adventure written by a friend of Ian Fleming, the plot of which Fleming was aware of and might even have contributed to, officially commissioned by Fleming's estate but never published... Unsurprisingly, this book has become something of an Eldorado for Bond-lovers. So what was *Per Fine Ounce*, exactly?

After Ian Fleming's death in 1964, British journalist John Pearson sat down to write a biography of the creator of James Bond. Pearson set about contacting as many people he could find who had known the novelist, asking for their recollections. On 6th June 1965, he wrote to Geoffrey Jenkins, a South African who had become friends with Fleming in the 1940s, when they had both worked at *The Sunday Times*.

Jenkins had returned to South Africa and become a thriller-writer – his first novel, *A Twist Of Sand*, published in 1959, sold three million copies worldwide.[1] Fleming thought highly of it – or at least valued Jenkins' friendship enough to praise it in print: 'Geoffrey Jenkins has the supreme gift of originality,' he wrote in *The Sunday Times*. '*A Twist of Sand* is a literate, imaginative first novel in the tradition of high and original adventure.'[2] In 1962, Fleming reviewed Jenkins' third novel *A Grue Of Ice*, also for *The Sunday Times*. Comparing him favourably to John Buchan, Hammond Innes and Geoffrey Household, he concluded that Jenkins was 'in the ranks of the great adventure writers'.[3]

It's not surprising Fleming raved about Jenkins – he knew the writer, and in many ways his work was similar to his own. This was noted by other publications: *Books and Bookmen* felt Jenkins' style combined 'the best of Nevil Shute and Ian Fleming',[4] while *The Times Literary Supplement* wrote: 'Ian Fleming is Geoffrey Jenkins' spiritual headmaster and Mr Jenkins stands in the not unenviable position of being Mr Fleming's most brilliant pupil'.[5] When he received Pearson's first letter in 1965, Fleming's pupil had four best-sellers under his belt – he would go on to write 12 more.

On 24th September 1965, Jenkins sent an eight-page typewritten reply to Pearson, in which he recounted his memories of Fleming, who he had met while he was on Lord Kemsley's Commonwealth Scholarship scheme:

> 'Later Lord Kemsley himself asked me to stay on and gave me a job in the Foreign Department, of which Fleming was the head.'[6]

Jenkins related how Fleming took him out to lunch early on in the job, he suspected out of duty, but that they quickly became friends: 'In the next eighteen months or so he had introduced me to many leading London clubs.'[7] According to Jenkins, Fleming was, unlike Bond, 'essentially an introvert'; nevertheless, he was surprised, on meeting his old friend for lunch at The Caprice in London in 1961, when they had both become best-selling authors, that Fleming was full of doubts about his creation: 'Fleming was gloomy; publishing and film worries were in his mind; he was searching for a theme for his next Bond, which was due the following spring, nine months away. "I have created a monster," he told me. "I have written every permutation of sex and sadism, and still the public wants more? What shall I write about?"'[8]

The result was *The Spy Who Loved Me*. But despite Fleming's dark mood, something triggered off the old spark between the two: 'In a moment we were kicking around – in a light-hearted, gay mood, completely in contrast to that of a few minutes before – the idea of making Bond a necrophile. Both of us threw our ideas into the melting-pot as they were minted; scene after scene built up, each more hilarious than the last, each more censorious than the last, until we found that most of the afternoon was gone and that we were the only diners left, with waiters standing by in patient protest: something which had happened many times before in the Fleet Street days.'[9]

In the next paragraph, Jenkins drops a bombshell. A few years before the Caprice lunch, he and Fleming had kicked around ideas about Bond altogether more seriously:

> 'I tried very hard to get him to come out to South Africa to write a James Bond set in this country. Twice he nearly came. I wrote him the outline of a plot which he thought had great possibilities (this was before *A Twist of Sand*) bringing in a secret/spy escape route through a magic lake

named Fundudzi in the Northern Transvaal, towards Mozambique. "I must know how everything smells, tastes and looks for myself in South Africa," he wrote to me. "Without them, it is not for me." On both occasions when he decided to come and see for himself, something arose and he postponed it.'[10]

Jenkins goes on to discuss Fleming's views on writing thrillers: expertise was essential, and could almost over-rule the need for a decent plot (Fleming apparently felt his own plots were thin). Jenkins says that at one of their last meetings Fleming had told him that he felt success had sapped him of energy and creativity, and also reveals that the writer's favourite city had been Hong Kong, on account of its vibrancy.

In his covering note for the letter, Jenkins asked Pearson if his Bond outline was in Fleming's papers, as he seemed to have mislaid it. 'It ran to about 25 pages of typescript, and [Fleming] was pretty keen on it.'[11]

On 1st October 1965, Pearson replied, thanking Jenkins for his 'splendid letter', which he had enjoyed hugely – especially the idea of making Bond a necrophile: 'he would have done it so well, too'. He added that he had found Jenkins' Bond outline, and asked if he should send it to him. 'Perhaps you should write it yourself now?'[12]

Unknown to Pearson, that idle comment would open up a hornet's nest. Encouraged by Pearson's enthusiasm, Jenkins replied to him on 6th October 1965, saying that he would appreciate seeing the outline again: 'Ian was very keen on it, as I mentioned, and we discussed it verbally at length and made quite a few changes. I know what was in his mind for it and the approach he contemplated.' He ended the letter by saying he would be in London in November – 'perhaps we could meet?'[13]

The two men did meet, on 2nd November 1965; the next day, Pearson wrote to Jenkins:

> 'I did enjoy meeting you last night, although I meant to buy you the whisky. You must let me do so properly before you go back to the sun.
> I hope that you write that book. Just reading your synopsis through I can understand why Ian got so excited about it, and you can't possibly allow such magnificent material to go to waste. Gold bicycle chains and baobab wood coffins. What else can the Bond-lover ask for?
> All best wishes,
> John Pearson.'[14]

Later that same November, Jenkins met with Charles Tyrrell of Glidrose Productions Limited, the corporate owners of the James Bond literary copyright and Bond film co-producer, Harry Saltzman, at Bucklersbury House in London to discuss the idea of him developing his outline into a book.[15] Glidrose were already considering commissioning 'continuation' Bond novels,[16] so a friend of Fleming's, and a best-selling thriller-writer to boot, appearing with a plot that Fleming had apparently considered writing himself may have initially seemed like a gift. The fact that John Pearson had found the outline in Fleming's papers proved Fleming had known about it – and had taken it seriously enough to keep it.

Jenkins' ideas certainly sound like promising material for a Bond adventure. Fundudzi is a real lake in the Zoutpansberg Region of South Africa; hidden in a valley, locals believe it is sacred and enchanted. A white crocodile and a huge python are said to live in the lake, guarding its ancestral spirits. Jenkins' 1973 novel *A Cleft Of Stars* is set in the region:

'It is primarily the home of the grotesque baobab trees, whose bulbous, purple-hued trunks reel across the arid landscape like an army of drunken Falstaffs, blown and dropsied with stored water...'[17]

Baobab trees are also seen as sacred in many parts of Africa, and are sometimes used as coffins: the bodies of important individuals are placed in a hollowed-out baobab trunk to symbolise the communion between the forces of the plant gods and the body of the deceased.[18]

Precisely what Jenkins had planned for the baobab coffins and gold bicycle chains is a mystery, but his pitch must have worked: Jenkins felt that Tyrrell and Saltzman were both very keen on the idea.[19]

Negotiations over the contract took months. Jenkins wanted his regular publisher Collins, rather than Cape, the Bond books' usual home; and Fleming's widow, Ann, became perturbed about the issue of 'the original copyright' – 'whatever that means,' Jenkins wrote.[20]

On 12th May 1966, Glidrose cabled Jenkins to tell him that they had agreed to grant him permission to write the book, and would get the contract drawn up with his London solicitors, Harbottle and Lewis.[21] However, it wasn't until 24th August 1966 that Harbottle and Lewis sent Jenkins a contract – and even this looks like it wasn't the final version. The covering letter mentions that Glidrose were making noises about adding a clause stating that Jenkins would not be entitled to profits from merchandising related to any film of his novel. The contract in Jenkins' papers is undated and unsigned, but does contain such a clause. It seems likely that in the autumn of 1966, Glidrose and Jenkins' solicitors wrangled over the small print. The contract we have states that Jenkins would be paid £5,000 on signing the contract and £5,000 on publication of the novel. He would also be entitled to half of Glidrose's 2.5-percent share of global profits of any film or serial adaptation (excepting merchandising). He had six months to write the manuscript, which had to be at least 65,000 words long. He was to send four copies of the finished draft to Glidrose, but there was a clause giving them the right to refuse to publish if they saw fit.[22]

Jenkins was not the only iron Glidrose had in the fire, however: Kingsley Amis was approached at least five months before Jenkins was sent his contract. Alarmed by several attempts to publish unlicensed Bond novels, the estate had decided to enter the fray by commissioning an official new Bond writer, and Amis was one of the authors under consideration.[23] He was an obvious candidate: as well as being one of Britain's most respected novelists, Amis was a self-confessed "Fleming addict".[24] Since Fleming's death, he had proof-read *The Man With The Golden Gun* and published two books about Bond (*The James Bond Dossier* and *Every Man His Own 007*, the latter under the pseudonym Bill Tanner).[25]

Ann Fleming was 'violently against' the idea of a continuation novel, and of Amis writing it, but Ian's eldest brother and Glidrose director Peter Fleming was in favour and he eventually won her round. On March 15th, 1966, he wrote a letter to her that concluded:

> 'As you know, I was originally less than lukewarm towards the idea of a Continuation Bond; but, having seen more of the ramifications and repercussions of this extraordinary market, I now feel strongly that the right thing to do is to tell Kingsley Amis to go ahead.'[26]

According to Peter Fleming's biographer Duff Hart-Davis, Glidrose were 'forced' to commission Jenkins as he had 'claimed in a letter to the board that his would be the only true continuation, because he had written the outline of the plot (set in South Africa) at Ian's request, and Ian had seen it and "indeed was most enthusiastic about it."'[27]

This suggests that Jenkins might have been aware that he wasn't the only writer being considered. It seems he became impatient with the amount of time it was taking for permission to be granted him, and told Glidrose he would write the book anyway. As Jenkins had letters from Fleming's biographer praising his synopsis and confirming that it had been in Fleming's possession, he might have been much harder to stop than the pirates the continuation idea was meant to suppress. Perhaps for this reason, Glidrose granted him permission to write the book, but kept the right to refuse publication.

WHEN JENKINS SUBMITTED *Per Fine Ounce* – probably in early 1967 – they exercised that right of refusal. Despite an exhaustive search of Jenkins' papers with the help of his son David, a small army of archivists and even a psychic, nothing of the final draft of *Per Fine Ounce* has yet been discovered. Four pages of an earlier draft of the novel have come to light, however.

The pages are numbered 86, 87, 88 and 89. Each contains numerous handwritten corrections and additions in the margin, and has one faint diagonal pencil mark through it. Jenkins may have later decided to abandon the scene, or end it differently, or (perhaps most likely) the pages were simply typed up again with all the corrections added, a clean proof to be copied and sent to Glidrose.

The scene takes place in M's office. Present are M, Bond and a financier called Sir Benjamin. Page 86 starts in the middle of a discussion between the three men:

> "'Expensive powder-puff – £137 millions," said M.
> Bond argued on. "This gas cylinder business wasn't big enough to kill the pound. It was bound to be discovered. I say it was meant to be discovered…'"[28]

In the first page and a half, Bond argues that an incident with some gas cylinders that M and Sir Benjamin feel was designed to knock the rate of the pound was merely a smokescreen, and that some gold flights from South Africa are someone's or some organisation's real target. Sir Benjamin admits that if the gold flights were downed, it would 'send sterling for the count'. Much discussion ensues about these gold flights, which are due to travel from Luanda to London via Angola and Las Palmas, helped along by CIA surveillance, American fighter planes from their base on Ascension Island and nuclear subs carrying surface-to-air missiles. 'Finger-on-the-tit stuff,' Bond murmurs.

Bond wants to return to South Africa (where, it seems, the cylinder incident took place), and have another look at the situation. M thinks this would be a waste his time, and refuses to authorise it – it's 'outside the province of the 00 Section'. Then it really heats up:

> 'Bond stood up, looking down from across the desk into the old sailor's face. "I'm sorry, sir."
> M put down his pipe. "Sorry about what, 007?" The voice was ominous.

"In just over two months, this department won't exist," he said. As he did so, he regretted the pain he saw in the face of the man whom he admired above anyone he knew. "You recalled me because the Treasury wanted help. Fair enough. But do you think you'll get any more than an appreciative minute for today's discovery? Do you really think they'll reprieve your department because of a couple of piddling things like soda-water syphon cylinders?"

"I am ordering you, 007." Bond heard the sharp intake of breath from Sir Benjamin behind him.

"And I," said Bond, "Am – for once – refusing that order…'"

Bond uses an extended gambling metaphor to argue his case – there are references to *chemin de fer*, and 'the click of the chips, the silver chandeliers and the quiet monotones of the croupiers' – and concludes: 'It's the man who has the nerve to climb in when the Casino tries to keep him away who breaks the bank'. M says that Bond has done that many times in the past and Bond says yes, he has – 'But I did it for your department.' When Sir Benjamin asks Bond if he intends to back no more than a hunch, Bond replies: 'To the point of resigning.'

As the excerpt – and the chapter – ends, a VC10 takes off to South Africa and we learn that 'James Bond, for the first time, was going on a mission without the blessing of M.'

THE SCENE ITSELF is expository – the usual Bond and M in the office set-up – and such scenes are rarely exciting. However, it's clear from these pages that Jenkins knew Bond. This wasn't just a friend of Ian Fleming's who wrote thrillers – he was clearly a Bond aficionado. This is evident in Bond's voice, the descriptions of M, and the general atmosphere. Aside from a few typos and the odd clumsy phrase, it feels like it could be an excerpt from a Fleming Bond novel. It is also ahead of its time: at least 14 years before John Gardner's *Licence Renewed*, Jenkins had the idea of disbanding the Double 0 Section, and 22 years before the film *Licence to Kill*, Bond went rogue.

So why was the book rejected? According to Peter Janson-Smith, Ian Fleming's literary agent and former chairman of Glidrose, *Per Fine Ounce* was rejected on the grounds that it wasn't up to par. 'Frankly,' he says, 'I thought it was extraordinarily badly written.'[29]

This seems at odds with the standard of the four draft pages and the four best-sellers Jenkins had published before 1966, two of which Ian Fleming had praised highly. 'There was a rumour going round that Jenkins was very good at creating plots but wasn't much of a writer, and that he had an editor at Collins who wrote his books up,' said Janson-Smith. 'When I read his Bond story, I could believe that rumour. It just wasn't good enough.'

Jenkins was a close friend of his publisher Sir Billy Collins, and sometimes took advice on small points from him (in much the same way Fleming did from William Plomer), but there is no evidence in Jenkins' notes, correspondence or drafts that Collins or anyone else was effectively writing his books on his behalf. Even if the rumour were true, Jenkins' previous books had all been best-sellers: did nobody consider editing Per Fine Ounce in the same way? Janson-Smith said he felt no editing could have saved the novel, but added: 'Possibly we were a little stricter with [continuation novels] in those days.'

Janson-Smith had a vague recollection that the book had had 'something to do with gold' – and that the plot had been 'rather good'. He said Ann Fleming had not been involved in its rejection – 'she played no part in editorial decisions'. And he had one other twist to the tale: he didn't believe that Glidrose (or Ian Fleming Publications, as the company is now called) would still have a copy of the book. 'They would have returned it to him,' he said firmly. This was because of the problem of plagiarism. Even while Fleming was alive, unsolicited typescripts had poured in to Glidrose – the standard practice was to return them, for fear of being sued later. As Glidrose didn't think Jenkins' novel was good enough to publish, Janson-Smith suggested, they would have no reason to keep it – and good reason to send it back, to help ensure that Jenkins didn't sue them for any similarities in any subsequent continuations. 'They would have sent a note saying the story was his to use again, but he just wouldn't be able to use Bond, M and so on.'

Indeed, the version of the contract Glidrose sent Jenkins that is now stored in his papers included precisely such a clause:

> 'If the New Bond Book offered by Glidrose for publication hereunder is rejected by Glidrose nothing herein contained shall prevent Geoffrey Jenkins from using elsewhere any part or the whole of the plot of such rejected New Bond Book and any of the characters appearing therein other than James Bond and the Bond characters.' [30]

It seems likely that Jenkins would have wanted to take Glidrose up on this. Writing a novel is no easy business, and why waste a plot you have already worked out? Many of Jenkins' books have similarities to and echoes of Fleming's work – could one of them be a reworked *Per Fine Ounce*? John Pearson was, unfortunately, unable to remember anything specific about the book, and had no firm memories of his correspondence and meeting with Jenkins in 1965.[31]

Some writers have speculated that the plot was about diamond-smuggling.[32] This is possible but, in the draft pages at least, it is about gold. Added to this are Jenkins' references to gold bicycle chains, Peter Janson-Smith's vague memory of 'something to do with gold', and that 'per fine ounce' is a common abbreviation of 'per Troy fine ounce', the standard unit of weight for gold. The standard unit of weight for diamonds is the carat. (Carats are also used for gold; this refers to the proportion of gold in an alloy, rather than the weight, and is now spelled "karat" in some countries to avoid confusion.)[33]

Jenkins' 1983 novel *The Unripe Gold* is about another precious metal: iridium. Set in the diamond mining town of Oranjemund in south-west Africa, it features a crazed German scientist who has discovered a ton of the extremely rare metal, which he intends to use to tip the balance of the Cold War. As in Fleming's *Thunderball*, a group of terrorists masquerade as prospectors. The town is protected by a Major Rive, the head of a security service employed by Consolidated Diamond Mines.[34] As a terrorist approaches the town's perimeter fence, the guard on duty mistakes him for Rive:

> 'What was bugging him tonight? Sneezer asked himself. Maybe one of his hunches – and no one could deny that on a famous occasion Major Rive's hunch had paid off when there had been a James Bond attempt to land a plane upcoast and fly out a parcel of stolen diamonds.'[35]

This appears to be a reference to an incident described by Ian Fleming in *The Diamond Smugglers*, which coincidentally was also used as the basis for the pre-titles sequence of an unfilmed screenplay adaptation of that book by the Australian writer Jon Cleary in 1964. [And that's the subject of the next chapter.]

In several of Jenkins' novels, the protagonists are ruthless Brits with naval backgrounds. *A Cleft Of Stars*' Guy Bowker has had commando training and served in the Royal Navy in the Second World War, while Ian Ogilvie, the hero of *The Watering Place of Good Peace* (1960), is a Scot who was crippled by a shark, also while in the Royal Navy. He joins an organisation constructing anti-shark barriers 'a fast car, a pretty girl, and half a dozen drinks' after his accident.[36]

The clearest echo of Bond, however, is Geoffrey Peace, the debonair and cruel-mouthed hero of *A Twist Of Sand* (1959) and *Hunter-Killer* (1966). The latter was the first novel Jenkins wrote after Fleming's death, and includes a wry and touching tribute to his old friend.

Published a year before the release of the film *You Only Live Twice*, the novel's narrator is John Garland (note the reversed initials), who was Geoffrey Peace's first mate in *A Twist of Sand*. Garland has not seen Peace for years when he suddenly receives a cable from his old friend asking him to come to meet him in Mauritius. Garland is a navigational expert, and Peace says he wants to collaborate with him on a system he has devised. But when Garland arrives, he finds that Peace is distracted. He wants to sail around some remote islands in the Seychelles used by one of his ancestors, a pirate – and when he's finished doing that, he decides to go spear-fishing. Garland is not pleased:

> 'My irritation with the whole affair increased when I found that I would have to stage back to Johannesburg via East Africa, and that the aircraft was an old flying-boat which only made the leisurely trip once a week. That meant a further delay of three days in the Seychelles. I cursed the soft languor of Limuria.'

As Garland has dinner in his hotel that night, a naval officer interrupts his meal and hands him a note, which says that Peace has been found dead in the water half a mile north of Frigate Island.

All this is told in flashback as Garland looks at Peace's coffin on board Peace's luxury yacht in Mahé. He is grief-stricken by the loss of someone he admired so much, dismayed by the publicity surrounding his death – elaborate preparations are underway to bury Peace at sea with full naval honours – and perversely angry that Peace died 'no more excitingly than an overfed businessman who drops dead after a dip at Ramsgate'.

Just a few pages into this novel, Jenkins made several references to both James Bond and Ian Fleming, some more obvious than others. The opening chapters are a clever spin on Fleming's 1960 short story *The Hildebrand Rarity*, published in the collection *For Your Eyes Only* in 1960. In that story, Bond was sent to Mahé by M to see if it would be feasible for the Admiralty to relocate its fleet base there from the Maldives:

> 'Bond's report, which concluded that the only conceivable security hazard in the Seychelles lay in the beauty and ready availability of the Seychelloises, had been finished a week before and then he had nothing to do but wait for the SS Kampala to take him to Mombasa. He was thoroughly sick of the heat and the dropping palm trees and the interminable conversation about copra.'

Like Bond, Peace goes spear-fishing; like Bond, Garland is forced to while away his time waiting for the weekly boat to East Africa. In a wry touch, in *Hunter-Killer* the British now have a missile base in the islands.

Fleming wrote *The Hildebrand Rarity* after visiting the Seychelles for the *Sunday Times* in 1958: he searched for buried pirate treasure on Fregaté, also known as Frigate Island (the hotel he stayed in, the Northolme, now has an Ian Fleming Suite.)

The remark about Ramsgate may be a reference to *Goldfinger*: James Bond stayed there before playing golf with the eponymous villain at the nearby Royal St George course in Sandwich – Ian Fleming died of a heart attack shortly after a meeting there.

Few people who read *Hunter-Killer* at the time would have been likely to have spotted these references – they are skilfully woven into the action. But I think there is another layer to these scenes that was entirely personal to Jenkins, and which related to his Bond synopsis. He had sent that to Fleming and suggested that he come out to South Africa to research and write it – in effect proposing a business partnership. In *Hunter-Killer*, the situation is reversed: it is Peace/Fleming who asks Garland/Jenkins to come out to see him for business. When Peace seems more intent on having fun than collaborating, Garland sourly begins to view what had been the chance to work with an old friend as a failed 'deal'. When Peace dies, he is racked with guilt about this. Was the opening of *Hunter-Killer* a metaphor for how Jenkins felt about his Bond collaboration with Fleming?

Perhaps to compensate, Jenkins said goodbye to Ian Fleming in his fiction. Garland watches Peace's steel coffin, 'shrouded by a tarpaulin', fired from a British destroyer's depth-charge mortar in the company of Peace's former boss, the Director of Naval Intelligence. Ian Fleming, of course, had been personal assistant to the DNI in the Second World War. A helicopter then hovers over Peace's grave and a huge wreath floats down at the end of a parachute.

Having given his newly Bonded version of Fleming this marvellous send-off, Jenkins then brings him back – and in a way that Fleming would surely have enjoyed. In the next scene, Garland visits the DNI in a cottage on Mahé, where he is living with a beautiful young Seychelloise called Adele. As the three of them talk, Garland senses someone approaching. It is, of course, Geoffrey Peace.

> 'I blinked in disbelief. Peace stood on the terrace in the same black rubber suit in which I had seen him in his coffin. A long diving-knife was in his hand. I tried to speak, but the words would not come...
> Mam'zelle Adele was still on my arm. Peace's greeting to her was level, comradely.
> 'Hello, Mam'zelle Adele.'
> She detached herself. 'Good evening, Commander. Was it a good trip?'
> 'Get me a drink and I'll tell you,' he replied.'[37]
> Over wine and turtle steak, the burial at sea is revealed to be a hoax by the DNI to persuade the US Air Force, the CIA and others that Peace is dead so he can embark on a secret mission involving a new type of space missile: 'the ultimate weapon'. Later in the novel, Peace introduces himself as "Peace – Commander Geoffrey Peace".

JENKINS' NOVELS OFTEN feature tough men scrabbling for a prize across harsh terrain – in Africa, the ocean or, particularly effectively in *A Grue Of Ice* (1962), Antarctica. None, however, feature Lake Fundudzi, gold flights, attempts to kill the pound or gas cylinders. Of them all, I think *A Cleft Of Stars* gives the best sense of what a Jenkins Bond novel might have been like. It shares an antecedent with *Diamonds Are Forever*: both books owe a debt to John Buchan's 1910 adventure *Prester John*, which concerns the tracking down of an illicit diamond pipeline in Africa. *A Cleft Of Stars*, which involves both diamonds and gold, is set in precisely the same region of South Africa as Jenkins' Bond outline from the '50s; the main character even spends some time hiding out in a hollowed-out baobab tree. It's a superb thriller: the descriptions of landscape and physical discomfort – Jenkins' trademarks – are exceptionally vivid and well drawn, and the tension builds to a highly Bond-like conclusion. Like many of Jenkins' novels, it would make a terrific film.

Jenkins was attracted to many of the same subjects as Fleming. Natural oddities abound in his work, as in *A Twist of Sand*, in which two characters see a 'double-sun', a phenomenon that had been recorded by meteorologists in 1957. He was fascinated by real-life mysteries: *Scend of The Sea* involves the search for the Waratah, a ship that sank without trace in 1909. Jenkins' villains also feel of the same stamp as Fleming's: *A Cleft Of Stars'* Doctor Manfred von Praeger keeps a hyena for a pet, while in *A Grue Of Ice* Carl Pirow is known as 'The Man With The Immaculate Hand' on account of an uncanny ability to imitate the fist of any ship's radio transmission. Jenkins' novels were meticulously researched, and packed with just the kind of schemes and scrapes Fleming loved. Fleming was right – Jenkins was a great adventure writer.

How to square that assessment with Glidrose's decision not to publish? Times, and attitudes, change: due to the enormous cultural influence of Fleming's creation, it's easy to forget that his novels were unusually digressive, leisurely and stylised in comparison to other thrillers of the time. Geoffrey Jenkins wrote straightforward adventure novels, sometimes short on style but always long on atmosphere and suspense. In the immediate wake of Fleming's death, it's perhaps unsurprising that Glidrose weren't keen – especially as a writer of the literary stature of Kingsley Amis was also interested in tackling Bond.

WE DON'T KNOW how Jenkins reacted to *Per Fine Ounce's* rejection - his son says he was very much "a closed shop" when it came to his professional life. Jenkins continued to write best-sellers, though, and the film world soon spotted his potential: *A Twist of Sand* was released by United Artists in 1968, directed by Don Chaffey. Richard Johnson – who had been Terence Young's favourite to play James Bond[38] – starred as Commander Geoffrey Peace, alongside Honor Blackman and Guy Doleman. Geoffrey Jenkins died in 2001, aged 81.

Could *Per Fine Ounce* have been a cracking Bond adventure? Jenkins' published novels and the four draft pages strongly suggest it might have been – but it may also have needed a sensitive editor to bring in some of Fleming's literary flair, an idea that would probably not have been attractive at the time. We might never know. David Jenkins is mystified as to why the manuscript of *Per Fine Ounce* is not in his father's papers: 'My dad kept everything.' Indeed, his papers include notes and drafts of all his novels, newspaper clippings, maps, pamphlets, publicity material, photographs, invitations to award ceremonies and hundreds of letters – even correspondence regarding a desk he commissioned. But, aside from the four draft pages, nothing more about Bond or Ian Fleming. We only have Geoffrey Jenkins' word that Ian Fleming approved of his story and contributed his own ideas to it – without the correspondence between the two men, it is impossible to gauge the exact extent of their collaboration, beyond the fact that Fleming had the outline. It might be that Jenkins destroyed the manuscript of *Per Fine Ounce*, or kept that and all his other Bond-related material in some place as yet unknown. For the moment, the search has been called off.

John Pearson's *The Life Of Ian Fleming* was published in 1966. The book ended with Fleming's death, making no mention of Per Fine Ounce. In his initial letter to Geoffrey Jenkins of 6th June 1965, Pearson had said his deadline for the book was Christmas of that year – as Jenkins did not get the go-ahead for his novel until August 1966 at the earliest, it may be that Pearson decided not to mention the book in case it did not pan out (as, indeed, it did not). In the introduction to the 2003 reprinting of the biography, Pearson wrote that some new information had come to light since 1966, but that on balance he stood by his original assessment.[39]

By May 1967, Amis had finished writing *Colonel Sun*.[40] The book was published the following year, and James Bond continuation novels have continued in some form since. But one can always wonder about what might have been. Jenkins' novels are all out of print now, but are easily found in second-hand bookstores and online. Why not try a couple – and then imagine the same author, who knew Fleming and his books well, writing a book about James Bond on a mission in South Africa, having handed in his resignation to M... And who knows? Perhaps, at the bottom of a drawer somewhere, this lost piece of Bond history is gathering dust – Eldorado may yet be waiting to be discovered.

Notes for this chapter:

1. 'Master of the adventure yarn passes on', *Daily Dispatch*, South Africa, November 15, 2001.
2. http://www.geoffrey-jenkins.co.za
3. Front and back covers of the 1966 Fontana edition.
4. Quoted in the back pages of several Jenkins novels: see, for example, Fontana, 1975, p223.
5. John Pearson begun his first letter to Geoffrey Jenkins (June 6, 1965): 'Dear Mr Jenkins, I worked with Ian at Kemsley's some time after you, and so made contact with the same spiritual headmaster, but never with the depth and success you seem to have done...' In his reply of September 24 1965, Jenkins quoted the part of the *TLS* review reproduced here.
6-11. Jenkins to Pearson, September 24 1965, Jenkins papers.
12. Pearson to Jenkins, October 1 1965, Jenkins papers.
13. Jenkins to Pearson, October 6 1965, Jenkins papers.
14. Pearson to Jenkins, November 2 1965, Jenkins papers.
15. Letter to Stanley Gorrie (Jenkins' accountant), March 22, 1966. Jenkins refers to the novel as *Per Fine Ounce* in this letter.
16. *Peter Fleming: A Biography* by Duff Hart Davis (Oxford University Press, 1987), pp374-5.
17. *A Cleft Of Stars* by Jenkins (Fontana, 1975), p20.
18. *Sacred Trees* by Nathaniel Altman (Sterling, 2000), p170.
19. Letter to Stanley Gorrie, March 22 1966, Jenkins papers.
20. Ibid.
21. Letter to Stanley Gorrie, May 13 1966, Jenkins papers.
22. Ibid.
23. *Peter Fleming: A Biography* by Duff Hart Davis (Oxford University Press, 1987), pp374-5.
24. Letter from Amis to Victor Gollancz on 1.05.1964, *The Letters of Kingsley Amis* edited by Zachary Leader (Miramax Books, 2001), p677.
25. It has been rumoured that Amis wrote or rewrote parts of this novel, but his letter to Tom Maschler of Jonathan Cape of 05.10.1964 (Leader, pp685-6) makes it clear he was simply asked to proof-read it.
26. *Peter Fleming: A Biography* by Duff Hart Davis (Oxford University Press, 1987), pp374-5.
27. Ibid.

28. This and the following passages are all from *Per Fine Ounce* draft pages, Jenkins papers.
29. This and subsequent quotes from interview with Janson-Smith, 25.02.2005.
30. Jenkins papers.
31. Interviews with Pearson, 25.02.2005 and 28.08.2005.
32. For example, *The Bond Files* by Anthony Lane and Paul Simpson, (Virgin Books, 2002), p433. One possible reason for the confusion might be that the only two books Fleming wrote that featured Africa were *Diamonds are Forever* and *The Diamond-Smugglers*.
33. *Precious Stones* by Max Bauer (Dover, 1968), p104, and *CRC Handbook of Materials Science* edited by Charles T Lynch, 1988, p21.
34. A similar job to Percy Sillitoe's for De Beers, both in real life and in *Diamonds are Forever*. See Chapter 2, *Uncut Gem*, for more.
35. *The Unripe Gold* (Fontana, 1973), p212.
36. *The Watering Place of Good Peace* (Fontana, 1974), p25.
37. *Hunter-Killer* (Fontana, 1973), p86.
38. Dana Broccoli interview on *Inside Dr No*, written and directed by John Cork, 2000.
39. *The Life of Ian Fleming* by John Pearson (Aurum Press, 2003), p8.
40. Amis to Philip Larkin, May 21 1967, Leader, p712.

Uncut Gem

A MAN RUNS across a beach, desperate to reach a plane at the far end of it. He hands something to the pilot just as it takes off. The plane rises into a bank of fog, whereupon it erupts into a ball of flame. The man rushes toward the crash, scrambling through the wreckage until his foot hits something. Looking down, he sees a small metal canister. He picks it up and fumbles it open. Diamonds spill into his hand...

If this sounds like the pre-titles sequence of a Bond film, it's not a coincidence. It *is* a pre-titles sequence, and it's from a screenplay based on one of Ian Fleming's books. For the past 45 years, its existence has remained unknown outside the small group of men who tried to film it.

I first became aware of the story when reading *The Letters of Kingsley Amis*. I was intrigued by a short letter he had sent fellow writer Theo Richmond in December 1965:

'I have been having a rather horrible time writing a story outline for one George Willoughby. Based on an original Fleming idea. Willoughby and the script-writer change everything as I come up with it. I gave W. the completed outline five days ago and he has been too shocked and horrified and despairing to say a word since. However, he has already paid me. (Not much.)'[1]

I smiled at the familiar writer's complaint, then stopped in my tracks. What 'original Fleming idea'? I'd never heard of it, and couldn't find any reference to it anywhere else. I decided to investigate. My first step was to contact Zachary Leader, Amis' biographer and the editor of his letters, to ask him if he had any idea where the outline might be. He wasn't sure, but put me in touch with the Huntington Library in California and the Harry Ransom Center in Texas, both of which hold Amis' papers. Researchers there sent me inventories of everything they held, and I started trying their patience by asking them to go through boxes that sounded as though they might conceivably contain the outline. After weeks of this, and feeling as though we had examined practically every scrap of paper Amis had saved, I called time. Wherever Amis' outline was, it didn't appear to be stored with the rest of his papers.

My attention turned to the other clue mentioned in Amis' letter: 'one George Willoughby'. And here I got a little luckier. Willoughby, I discovered, was a Norwegian who had moved to London and become a medium-sized fish in the British film industry. In 1951, he had been an associate producer on *Valley Of Eagles*, directed and co-written by Terence Young and filmed at Pinewood, the studio owned by The Rank Organisation, at that time Britain's largest film company. Young went on to direct several of the Bond films, shooting large parts of them at Pinewood.

In 1954, Willoughby had been an associate producer on *Hell Below Zero*, an adaptation of a Hammond Innes novel made by Warwick Films. Warwick was a company founded by Irving Allen and Albert 'Cubby' Broccoli, and it specialised in making relatively inexpensive but exciting action films. In 1962, Cubby Broccoli would part ways with Allen and form a new company, Eon, with Harry Saltzman. One of the scriptwriters for *Hell Below Zero* was Richard Maibaum, who Broccoli would take with him: he would go on to have a hand in the scripts to over a dozen Bond films.

Finally, in 1957 George Willoughby had been the associate producer on *Action Of The Tiger*, another Terence Young-directed film, this one featuring a young Sean Connery. So he had worked with three of the men who would become key players in the Bond franchise: Broccoli, Young and Maibaum. But while this was intriguing, I was no closer to finding the outline of the 'original Fleming idea' Amis had written for Willoughby.

But after several months of consulting authors' societies, literary agents and film libraries, I finally found what I was looking for. To my surprise, a lot of the story had been hiding in plain sight since 1989 in a book called *In Camera*, a volume of memoirs by Richard Todd.

DURING THE SECOND World War, Todd had served in the Army's 6th Airborne Division – he was the first man of the main force to parachute out over Normandy on D-Day. After the war, he had become one of Britain's biggest film stars. He was nominated for an Oscar for *The Hasty Heart* in

1949, after which he went on to play several leading roles, including starring opposite Marlene Dietrich in Alfred Hitchcock's *Stage Fright*. However, he is probably best remembered today for playing Wing Commander Guy Gibson in the classic war film *The Dam Busters*.

Like Willoughby, Todd had also worked with many of the people who were to become central to the James Bond series. Although he was a contract player with Rank's main rivals, the Associated British Picture Corporation (ABPC), who were based at Elstree Studios, he sometimes worked on 'loan-out' for Rank, for example on *Venetian Bird*, an adaptation of a Victor Canning thriller.

He had also made a film for Cubby Broccoli: *The Hellions*, a quasi-Western shot in South Africa in 1961. The following year, he was one of the star-studded cast of *The Longest Day*, an adaptation of Cornelius Ryan's account of D-Day. Todd played Major John Howard, who had been his superior officer on the day in real life. On the set in Caen in France, he met a 'rather shy' young Scottish actor with a small part in the film: Sean Connery.[2]

In April 1962, while Cubby Broccoli and Harry Saltzman were busy finalizing their contract with United Artists for the first Bond film, *Dr No*[3], Todd was informed that his contract with ABPC would not be renewed the following year. This was a body blow: it meant that he would now have to fend for himself in the jungle of Britain's rapidly declining film industry, which was under increasing pressure from Hollywood. But he had at least one iron in the fire, in the form of his friend George Willoughby, who 'had secured an option on the screen rights of an Ian Fleming book, *The Diamond Story* [sic], an intriguing exposé of illicit diamond-buying in Afica and of the undercover activities of agents who worked to counteract it'.[4]

So here it was: this was the elusive project Amis had been working on. *The Diamond Smugglers* was Fleming's first foray into full-length non-fiction, and apart from the guidebook Thrilling Cities remains the only one of his books not to have been filmed. It was originally published in 1957, collecting a series of articles in *The Sunday Times* in which Fleming had explored the shady world of diamond trafficking. A new edition of the book was published in 2009, with an introduction by Fergus Fleming, the writer's nephew. 'The success of Bond tends to eclipse Ian Fleming's other talents,' he tells me. 'It's often forgotten that he was also an accomplished journalist, travel writer and children's author.'[5]

Ian Fleming had become fascinated by the illegal trade in gemstones in 1954, when he had discovered that the world's biggest diamond-seller, De Beers, had set up its own private intelligence agency, the International Diamond Security Organisation, to try to combat it. IDSO was run by Sir Percy Sillitoe, who had previously been the head of MI5. Fleming met with Sillitoe and other diamond industry insiders, and used much of what he learned as background material for *Diamonds Are Forever*, largely set in the United States.[6]

Three years later, Fleming was drawn back into the world of diamonds. IDSO had blocked several plots by international criminal networks to bring diamonds illegally out of the mines of South Africa, Sierra Leone and elsewhere, and had been disbanded. Sillitoe, irritated that he and the organization had not been given more credit for their successes, decided to publish a book about it. His intention was for it to be a sequel to his 1955 memoir *Cloak Without Dagger*, and with that in mind he commissioned one of IDSO's senior agents, John Collard, to ghost-write an account.

Collard was an old hand in the espionage game. He had been in MI5 in the early part of the Second World War, but had then moved to the counter-intelligence agency MI11, becoming its head by 1946. He then rejoined MI5 and played a major role in the capture and conviction of the 'atomic spy' Klaus Fuchs, before heading off to South Africa to join IDSO.[7]

Collard revisited his and other agents' reports and wrote the book. Sillitoe sent the manuscript to Denis Hamilton at *The Sunday Times* for his view; Hamilton liked it, but Leonard Russell on the paper felt that a professional journalist would be able to spice it up. They suggested that Ian Fleming, who worked for the paper, interview Collard with the aim of producing a series of articles. All involved agreed, and so in early April 1957 Fleming took an Air France Caravelle to Tangiers to meet John Collard. The two men quickly established a rapport, and Fleming started work.[8]

This mainly consisted of editing and redrafting the original manuscript. Collard had detailed the organisation's frustrations, failures and successes in clear, lively prose, and it probably would have sold well had it been published as it was. But it was no thriller. Fleming went through the text, cutting anything he felt was dull or overly complicated and heightening the most exciting passages as only he knew how. He also adapted information from Collard's source material: one IDSO agent's report in Collard's papers has 'Passage omitted I.F.' and 'Name omitted I.F.' all over it in Fleming's distinctive scrawl.[9]

The biggest change Fleming made was not to the content, but to the perspective. Collard had written the book as though Sillitoe were the narrator. Fleming kept most of Collard's material, but rewrote it so that he, Ian Fleming, became the narrator, the intrepid investigative journalist flying out to Tangiers to interview the mysterious hero of the tale, who he made Collard instead of Sillitoe.

This switch was clever in several ways. Firstly, Sillitoe was at that point nearly 70 years old, and was not nearly as compelling a subject as Collard, who was in his mid-forties and therefore a man with whom readers could more readily identify. Sillitoe was largely a desk man, while Collard had seen extensive action in the field, both with MI5 and with IDSO – indeed, he wrote of his own actions in the third person throughout his manuscript. Sillitoe was the M figure of the organisation, and Fleming must have realized that the public would be drawn to someone more like Bond.

This shift of focus from Sillitoe to Collard allowed Fleming to create something more reminiscent of his own famous thrillers, as well as to add some local colour and texture. The framing device of the interview allowed Fleming to break up Collard's long passages of close exposition about the diamond industry with some of his own brand of intrigue, bringing in references to life in Tangier, other spies such as Richard Sorge and Christine Granville and, of course, James Bond.

Either prompted by others or on his own initiative, Fleming also gave several of the people featured in the book different names, including Collard. The book discussed at length how IDSO had foiled several unscrupulous gangs, so there might have been some concern about blowback following publication. For Collard, Fleming chose the rather Bond-ish 'John Blaize' – in the germ of a scene in one of his notebooks, he had had Miss Moneypenny suggest 'Major Patrick Blaize' as a cover name for Bond.[10]

Fleming portrayed Collard/Blaize as a quieter, shyer character than Bond, although readers would learn that he owned 24 fine white silk shirts and intended to spend 48 hours gambling intensively in Monte Carlo 'to wash the last three years and the African continent out of his system'.[11]

In 1965, Leonard Russell wrote to Collard to ask him about his recollections of Fleming for a biography he was writing of him with John Pearson – Pearson eventually took over the job completely – and Collard gave a detailed account of how the book had come about and how he had met Fleming. In much the same way he'd ghost-written himself into Sillitoe's memoir, he also wrote this up in the third person. He reveals the week included them playing golf together and attending parties, and that they kept in touch in subsequent years:

> 'In the bar at the Royal St Georges or Rye Golf Club, they could sometimes be seen having a private yarn.'[12]

The two men evidently got on well in Tangiers, but Fleming's presentation of their meetings in the book is largely fiction. No doubt he asked Collard for clarification on some points, but his work was largely editorial: he took passages from Collard's book, rearranged and simplified them, and then had 'Blaize' speak them aloud while he, Fleming, supposedly leaned in and listened, interjecting occasional questions. In this way, the book took on the tone of a fascinating secret story being told in a darkened corner of a bar in the tropics, automatically giving it more vigour. Fleming could probably have done most of this work in London – but then, that wouldn't have been as exciting, or got him a few days' golf and partying in Tangiers.

To pre-empt any legal difficulties, Fleming sent proofs of his version of the book to The Diamond Corporation, De Beers' distribution arm in London. The move didn't work. Although the company initially appeared pleased with the text, it later took exception to several elements, and Fleming was forced into rewrites.[13] But finally, in September 1957, the articles began to be serialised in *The Sunday Times*. Readers learned about 'Monsieur Diamant', a 'big, hard chunk of a man with about ten million pounds in the bank'. Outwardly a respectable entrepreneur, his diamond-fencing activities had made him 'the biggest crook in Europe, if not in the world'. Another episode concerned a bravado attempt to fly 1,400 stolen diamonds out of Chamaais Beach in South-West Africa, which failed when the plane crashed on take-off.

The articles were collected to form a book, titled *The Diamond Smugglers*, which was published in November with an introduction by Collard (under the Blaize pseudonym). The book didn't differ a great deal from the manuscript Collard had originally written, but it had been souped up, texture had been added and, above all, Fleming's name had been appended to it. As a result, it received a level of marketing almost equal to that afforded to the Bond novels at the time.[14]

Fleming was happy with his scoop, but not entirely satisfied with the way the project had turned out. On the fly-leaf of his own copy of the book, now stored at Indiana University's Lilly Library, he noted:

> 'This was written in 2 weeks in Tangiers, April 1957. The name of the IDSO spy is John Collard. Sir Percy Sillitoe sold the story to the Sunday Times & I had to write it from Collard's M.S. It was a good story until all the possible libel was cut out. There was nearly an injunction against me &

the Sunday Times by De Beers to prevent publication of the S. T. serial. Rightly, they didn't like their secrets being sold by an employee. Lord Kemsley & Collard shared the profits of this – a third each, which was a pity as I sold the film rights to Rank for £12,500. It is adequate journalism but a poor book & necessarily rather "contrived" though the facts are true.'[15]

Perhaps as a result of his irritation at the suppression of some of the story's more exciting aspects, Fleming's view was overly pessimistic. The fact that Rank was prepared to pay a sizeable amount for the rights to a compilation of newspaper articles he had written in a fortnight was a sign of the growing interest in his work from the film industry. In 1954, Gregory Ratoff had taken a six-month option on his first novel, *Casino Royale*, for $600, and shortly after that CBS had bought the television rights to the same book for $1,000. The following year, Rank had snapped up the rights to *Moonraker* for £5,000. *Casino Royale* was rapidly made into an hour-long TV adaptation, with Barry Nelson as James 'Jimmy' Bond and Peter Lorre as Le Chiffre. Rank's *Moonraker* film never got off the ground.[16]

Rank was, initially at least, keen to publicise the fact that it had bought the rights to the book. *The Bookseller* noted that it had bought the rights for 'an unusually high figure', and had 'commissioned Ian Fleming to prepare the film treatment'[17], and '*The Diamond Smugglers* Story' was included in Rank's programme for 1958 along with *The Thirty-Nine Steps* and *Lawrence of Arabia* (both of those were prematurely announced, being released in 1959 and 1962 respectively). But 1958 passed, and the film didn't materialize.

THAT'S THE TRADITIONAL story of *The Diamond Smugglers*, mentioned in passing in dozens of books and articles. A slightly obscure Fleming work, not featuring James Bond. A success, but not one of his greater ones. The film rights sold, but no film made. Case closed.

Well, not quite. There *were* attempts to film *The Diamond Smugglers*, serious and prolonged attempts, as Todd's memoir showed. I contacted the actor's agent, but was told that due to frailty and a hazy memory he didn't feel he could add to what he had already written. This was understandable: Todd was approaching ninety and, unknown to me, suffering from cancer. I had by now also contacted John Collard's family, who kindly provided me with a great deal of material, including both his relevant correspondence from the time and the original manuscript of his book. Adding this to the information in Todd's memoirs and other sources, I started to piece together the rest of the story.

Willoughby set up his own production company in 1959, and at some point between then and 1962 obtained the film rights to *The Diamond Smugglers*. In a letter to a former colleague in 1965, John Collard wrote that he had met Willoughby 'about five years ago at the request of Ian Fleming'.[17]

From subsequent events, it seems that Rank may have told Willoughby that they had given up on trying to adapt the book, but that if he could put together the elements of a commercially viable film, they would distribute it. They later did just that with another Willoughby production, *Age of Innocence*, which had featured Lois Maxwell and Honor Blackman.

Todd and Willoughby became partners in 1962, and set to work: Derry Quinn, who had worked as a story supervisor on *Chase A Crooked Shadow*, a thriller Todd had made in 1958, was hired to write a treatment. As well as Todd's contacts within the industry and star power – presumably the original intention was for him to play Blaize – the actor also knew South Africa. While making *The Hellions*, he had been struck by the potential for a film industry there: it had widely varying scenery and climate, a lot of investors looking for overseas outlets, and a large pool of English-speaking actors.[18]

As *The Diamond Smugglers* took place in that part of the world, Todd now returned to his South African contacts, inviting to London Ernesto Bisogno, a businessman he had met on his *Hellions* trip who had dabbled in small-scale film production and was now forming a production company in Johannesburg. Bisogno was accompanied by an official of the South African Industrial Development Corporation, who Todd had also met the previous year. Their reactions to the project were apparently very favourable, and Todd was optimistic that he would be able to persuade ABPC to distribute the film once it was made. However, work on the screenplay was slow, with Todd's flat becoming 'a charnel-house of abandoned drafts and screen treatments'.[19] Fleming's book was essentially a series of unconnected episodes: crafting an exciting, coherent and commercial script from them would prove no easy task.

In April 1963, a full year after starting work on the project, the two men had a breakthrough: John Davis, the head of Rank, put them in touch with Earl St John, who was in charge of productions at Pinewood. St John had been an executive producer on *Passionate Summer*, a film Willoughby had produced in 1958. He liked their pitch, and as a result Rank funded a trip to South Africa and South-

West Africa (now Namibia) in May 1964 to scout locations in which to set the screenplay for *The Diamond Smugglers*.[20]

BY NOW A new writer had arrived on the scene: the Australian Jon Cleary, then best known for his novel *The Sundowners*, the film of which had starred Robert Mitchum and Deborah Kerr and had been nominated for five Academy Awards. Now in his nineties, he still vividly recalls his work on *The Diamond Smugglers*. 'My doctor says my body is ninety but my head's fifty,' he laughs when I speak to him on the phone from his home in Sydney. According to Cleary, Rank had originally bought the rights to the book because of Fleming's name. 'They disowned it when they realised it was a grab-bag of pieces he had written one wet weekend. There was no story. So they put it on the shelf.'[21]

But now *The Diamond Smugglers* had another shot. It was not only back on Rank's radar – they were putting up money to develop it. Accompanying Todd, Willoughby and Cleary on the trip to Africa was the American director Bob Parrish, who, according to Cleary, had agreed to direct the film subject to a satisfactory script being developed. Cleary and Parrish both lived in London and knew each other; Cleary says Parrish put him forward for the project. Parrish, who had won an Oscar as an editor, had directed an adaptation of Geoffrey Household's *A Rough Shoot*, from a script by Eric Ambler, and *Fire Down Below*, co-produced by Cubby Broccoli.

'We landed in Johannesburg on a Sunday afternoon,' Cleary remembered. 'There were three thousand people there to meet us at the airport! We stayed in the Langham Hotel, which was the place to be. Everything was laid on for us, and all kinds of avenues of research were opened – I knew nothing about diamonds. One day, a European woman – Contessa something-or-other – turned up at my hotel room to discuss the business, and emptied her chamois bag, spilling diamonds onto the table. It was about three or four million Rand, just sitting there!'

After spending a few days in South Africa, where they scouted locations in Johannesburg, M'Tuba'Tuba and Pretoria, the group flew to South-West Africa's capital, Windhoek. They were shown around by Jack Levinson and his wife Olga, who lived in a castle-like residence that had been built for the Commander-in-Chief when the country had been a German colony. The Levinsons were ideal guides for their mission: as well as being the city's mayor, Jack was also a lithium entrepreneur who had discovered diamonds on the Skeleton Coast, while Olga had recently published a history of the country.[22]

By now, the Bond films were big business, and with the release of *Goldfinger* in September, about to become a global phenomenon. Was the intention to leverage Fleming's material into a Bond-style plot? Not according to Cleary: 'It was always going to be much more realistic than the Bond films. We wanted to make use of the fact that we had these remote, exotic locations, but craft something much more down-to-earth, that nobody had seen before.'

Cleary, like Derry Quinn before him, was desperately looking for a way to connect the disparate elements of Fleming's book into an exciting plot. In South-West Africa, he finally hit upon an idea. 'Bob liked it. We told Richard – it would involve him being the villain, for a change. He jumped at it. The idea was for Steve McQueen to play the lead. I've forgotten who they wanted for the girl, but it was one of the top stars.'

McQueen, who had become well known after *The Magnificent Seven* in 1960, had just made *The Great Escape*, which had catapulted him to greater fame. Whether or not he would have been interested or available for *The Diamond Smugglers* is another question, but it's fascinating to think of him in a Fleming adaptation.

Cleary's original idea for the script was based on a story he had heard while the team were scouting the Skeleton Coast, about a man who sets up a model aeroplane club in the De Beers'-protected town Oranjemund, and then uses the model planes to try to smuggle some diamonds out. Fired up with the potential of this idea, Cleary 'went away and wrote a screenplay'. I ask him to repeat this to be certain I've heard correctly. There are no references to a completed screenplay in Todd's memoirs – or anywhere else. A script of an unfilmed Ian Fleming book, written in the Sixties by a well-known novelist, with funding by Rank… well, that would be something. 'Did you keep a copy?' I ask quietly. Cleary chuckles. 'I'm afraid I've never been a hoarder,' he says, and my heart sinks. He tells me that the State Library of New South Wales has his papers, but that they often call, begging him to send them his latest manuscript 'before I throw it out'.

This doesn't sound hopeful, but I contact the library anyway. And they have it. After obtaining permission from Cleary and his literary agency, I am sent a copy. I crack it open, and stare at the title page with amazement. 'The Diamond Smugglers by Ian Fleming. Draft screenplay by John Cleary.' I had gone looking for Amis' story outline, and had instead found a completed screenplay.

THE SCRIPT IS dated October 28 1964, and is 149 pages long. It begins:

> 'EXT. BEACH. SOUTH WEST AFRICA. EARLY MORNING.
> We open on a LONG SHOT of a desert, grey-blue and cold looking in the dawn light...'[23]

The protagonist has been renamed: instead of John Blaize, he is now Roy O'Brien, a tall, quiet American secret agent who is sent to a diamond mine in Johannesburg under cover as a pilot. His mission: to infiltrate and break up a ring of smugglers preparing to make a huge deal with the Red Chinese. O'Brien reads very much as though written with McQueen in mind. We are told he is 'marked with the sun and the scars of a man who has spent a good deal of his life in the outdoors' and that 'he was a boy once quick to smiles' but is now 'a man who has seen too much of sights that did not provoke laughter'. He is quick-witted, laconic, but very likeable.

We first meet him in Amsterdam, where he is staking out Vicki Linden, a beautiful young South-West-African diamond-smuggler of German descent. She is reminiscent of the character Tiffany Case in Fleming's novel *Diamonds Are Forever*, but somewhat softer and more naive (without being irritating). He follows Vicki to South Africa, and she tells him her ambition is to have a diamond 'for every day in the week'. He asks how far she has got in this and she wrinkles her nose and replies 'Only Monday', to which he retorts: 'Give me the chance and I'll try and dig up Tuesday for you.'

Despite the change from Blaize to O'Brien and the addition of new characters, Cleary's screenplay is remarkably faithful to the tone of Fleming's book, and takes a lot of cues from it. Cleary used locations, incidents, technical information and a lot of other elements and ideas from the book, and wove a thriller plot around them. The opening sequence is clearly inspired by the failed attempt to fly diamonds out from Chamaais Beach, although this time the plane doesn't simply crash but explodes mid-air. China's increasing interest in the illegal diamond trade, discussed at several points in the book, becomes the political backdrop of the plot; the description of security measures employed by mining companies is dramatised in a scene in which O'Brien is X-rayed; like Collard/Blaize, he makes use of a safe house in Johannesburg's back streets; and so on.

It is a very different beast to the Bond films. There are no nuclear warheads or hidden lairs: it is, as Cleary says was the intention, a gritty, down-to-earth thriller. Nevertheless, there are some suitably baroque and Fleming-esque touches. One of the villains is a diamond-smuggler called Cuza, who weighs over four hundred pounds 'but walks with a delicate step' and likes eating chocolates: 'Stone-bald, he wears dark glasses; a balloon head rests on a balloon body; he could be a clown or a killer.'

Cuza and his black sidekick Daniel work out of a windswept drive-in cinema projectionist's office. In one memorable scene, Daniel stalks O'Brien with a sniper rifle from his position on a catwalk running along the top of the cinema screen.

Cuza is in competition with a villain in a similar mould to Fleming's: Steven Halas is a wealthy German South-West-African businessman who likes giving lavish parties (at which he serves Bollinger '55) and taking photographs of big game, but beneath the veneer of sophistication he is greed personified. However, the real villain of the piece is revealed in the final act to be Ian Cameron, a womanising Scot who is the mine's field manager, and who is gently reminiscent of both Bond and Fleming. This, presumably, is the role that had been earmarked for Todd.

As well as drawing incidents and ideas from Fleming's book, the script is faithful to its tone, especially in its evocation of the sticky climate of fear and temptation permeating a diamond mining community. The shabbiness of O'Brien's accommodation provokes the script's one direct reference to Fleming's best-known creation, when his colleague Spaak is amused at its unsuitability and asks what has become of spies who only operate in five-star hotels. 'You need a nice low number,' O'Brien replies, 'Like 007. Whoever heard of a spy called 42663-stroke-12568?' 'What's that?' asks Spaak. 'My social security number,' comes the dry reply.

Highlights include two brutal hand-to-hand fights, one of which ends with the death of the monstrous Cuza, and a climactic car chase, which happens during an elephant stampede.

All told, the script is a cracker: a taut thriller with believable characters, snappy dialogue and a compelling plot. Its strongest features are its evocation of the Skeleton Coast – you can almost feel the dust and the dirt of this place that 'breeds seals, jackals and madmen', as one character describes it – and the subtle shading of the relationship between O'Brien and Vicki. Cleary also added some extra spice to the traditional police/spy story with elements of the Western and film noir, in a manner occasionally reminiscent of Orson Welles' *A Touch Of Evil*. His script is free of the troublesome plot holes, inconsistent characterisation and mixed tones common in many films of the time.

According to Todd's memoirs, in the summer of 1965 Rank signed an option to buy and produce the film, while on 14 June of that year, Willoughby wrote to John Collard to tell him that the production looked like it was back on the table:

> 'You may recollect that we met a few years ago in connection with the proposed production of a film based on Ian Fleming's "The Diamond Smugglers". Due to various circumstances at the time, these plans did not materialise. It is now a possibility that I shall be able to set up a production on this subject.'[24]

The letter is headed 'Willoughby Film Productions Limited' with an address in Sackville Street in London – but next to it Willoughby typed another address for Collard to reply to: Pinewood Studios, Iver Heath, Bucks.

Willoughby was contacting Collard again because he wanted his permission to use the character of John Blaize (the name O'Brien seemingly having been dropped). As a sweetener, he offered Collard a role as a technical adviser to the production.

Collard replied that De Beers should be consulted about the latest plans for the film, and asked for more details about it: would it be a documentary sticking closely to the book, or partly fictional?[25] On 21 June, Willoughby wrote to Collard again, writing that the film he had in mind was a 'feature entertainment', which would necessitate departing from Fleming's book, as that had mainly consisted of 'a number of incidents without a dramatic story line or link'. He understood that Collard might feel they were straying too far from the facts, but gave a surprising precedent for it:

> 'Fleming himself wrote for the Rank Organisation, a film treatment on this subject and although he used the name of

John Blaize for the hero, his treatment had, nevertheless, very little to do with the actual articles he wrote for the "Sunday Times".'[26]

This is the first mention of the existence of a film treatment for *The Diamond Smugglers* by Ian Fleming since *The Bookseller's* report of its commissioning in 1957 – but it would not be the last. On 1 September 1965, Collard received a letter from B.J. Rudd, an old acquaintance, who had enclosed a small cutting from *The Sun* from 25 August, titled 'Fleming film':

> 'An 18-page outline for a film about illicit diamond-buying written by Ian Fleming, creator of James Bond, is to be turned into a £1,200,000 film.'[27]

Collard and Willoughby, meanwhile, continued to correspond, with the producer revealing two new pieces of information in a letter on 27 August: a script was being completed by yet another writer, Anthony Dawson ('who lives not far from you in Sussex') and that the protagonist's surname had now been changed from Blaize to Blaine, to avoid confusion with Modesty Blaise.[28]

For anyone familiar with the James Bond films, the reference to Anthony Dawson is almost surreal: could this be the British character actor who had played Professor Dent in *Dr No* and who had been the presence (although not the voice) of arch-villain Ernst Stavro Blofeld in both *From Russia With Love* and *Thunderball*? It would seem so. Terence Young, who directed all three of those Bond entries, cast Dawson in several of his films, including *Valley of Eagles* and *Action of the Tiger*, both of which had had as associate producer one George Willoughby. It seems implausible that there were *two* Anthony Dawsons who worked on Ian Fleming projects in the Sixties, and that Willoughby collaborated with both. Dawson's son confirms that his father lived in Sussex during this period, and wrote several film scripts.[29] Unfortunately, he wasn't able to locate any material relating to *The Diamond Smugglers*.

A few weeks later, Barbara Bladen, a critic at the *San Mateo Times* in California, reported breathlessly on the film in her column:

> 'We'll have to start getting used to someone else playing James Bond in the Ian Fleming stories! Sean Connery has gone back to being Sean Connery and the Fleming pictures roll on. Latest before the cameras is "The Diamond Spy" on location in South Africa, Amsterdam and the Baltic coast of Germany. Richard Todd will play the slick agent. The author first wrote the book as a series of newspaper articles in 1957 and came out in book form as "The Diamond Smugglers."'[30]

The changing of the protagonist from a newly coined character to the world-famous James Bond is probably either Willoughby or Bladen's hyperbole – perhaps even a way around the fact that they had not yet resolved what to call the character. The locations listed are intriguing: South Africa and Amsterdam were both featured in Cleary's 1964 screenplay, but the Baltic coast of Germany was not. Could there have been another script by this time – or did Willoughby merely have an idea for one?

The title *The Diamond Spy*, which now started appearing in the press, did not please John Collard. On 3 January 1966, he wrote to Willoughby at Pinewood:

> 'If the revised title is seriously proposed, I am afraid that as far as I am concerned the film will start off on the wrong foot, whether it is described as fictional or coincidental, and the object of this letter is to advise you in the friendliest

possible manner to bear in mind my personal interest and the need to consider the risk of libel.'[31]

In a more placatory hand-written postscript, Collard explained that Fleming had originally planned on calling his book *The Diamond Spy*, but had changed it at Collard's request: 'The description "spy" carries with it a derogatory meaning,' he explained to Willoughby, 'and quite apart from its inappropriate use to describe "Blaize", I myself take strong exception to it.' The word 'spy' was often used in books and films at the time, and Fleming had of course used it in one of his titles, but Collard had worked for MI5, and in that and other intelligence agencies, the word was usually used to refer to informants and traitors.

Collard's letter seems to have been the first between the two men since August 1965, but it begun another flurry of correspondence. Willoughby immediately tried to reassure Collard that *The Diamond Spy* was merely a working title, which they were using 'because this is the title Fleming used for his story-line'. He invited him to lunch the next time he was in London to tell him more about the film.[32]

By now, Willoughby had hired Kingsley Amis as a 'special story and script consultant'. This news was reported in the American film industry magazine *Boxoffice* in January 1966:

> 'Kingsley Amis, novelist, critic and authority on the work of Ian Fleming, creator of James Bond, has been engaged as special story and script consultant on the new £11/4 film of Fleming's "The Diamond Spy", it was announced last week by British producer George Willoughby. The film, to be made early next year by Willoughby, in association with Richard Todd's independent company, is based on a story outline written by Ian Fleming but never completed by him. This outline was drafted by Fleming following his own investigations into international diamond smuggling, which

he wrote up as a series of articles for a Sunday newspaper in 1957. Later, these articles were collected and published in book form under the title of "The Diamond Smugglers".[33]

Now Amis, author of the recently published "James Bond Dossier", has been called in as a Fleming expert to develop the story, characters, situations and incidents so as to give "The Diamond Spy" film an authentic Fleming flavor. When he has completed this task, W. H. Canaway, who wrote the script of "The Ipcress File", will take over all the material, from which he will write the final screenplay.'[33]

This article repeated some material that had been published in *Boxoffice* in the same column a few months earlier[34], but the screenwriters' names were new – and brought a significant amount of prestige and experience to the table. *The IPCRESS File*, which had been produced by Harry Saltzman and featured the talents of several other Bond alumni, had been a great success, and Amis' status as a Fleming 'expert' would receive another push later the same month, when it was announced that he had been commissioned to write the first James Bond novel since Fleming's death.

On January 27 1966, Willoughby wrote to Collard to finalise the details of a meeting they were both to attend in London on 4 February:

> 'Thos [sic] present at the meeting, in addition to myself, will be Mr Kenneth Hargreaves of Anglo Embassy Productions Ltd., and Mr David Deutsch of Anglo Amalgamated Film Distributors.'[35]

It seems Willoughby had found yet new partners. Anglo Embassy was the English arm of Joseph E Levine's Embassy Pictures, which had produced *Zulu* and *The Carpetbaggers*. Levine would go on to produce *The Graduate*, *The Producers* and *The Lion In Winter*. Anglo Amalgamated's main claim to fame was the *Carry On* films, and in 1964 it had distributed *The Masque of The Red Death*, which Willoughby had associate-produced. But it was becoming increasingly high-brow, backing the first features of both John Boorman (*Catch Us If You Can*, released in 1965), and Ken Loach (*Poor Cow*, released in 1968). It had also released the highly controversial *Peeping Tom* in 1960.

On January 31, John Collard received a letter from Glidrose Productions: the owners of the James Bond literary copyright. It was from Beryl Griffie-Williams, 'Griffie', who had been Ian Fleming's secretary. She enclosed a newspaper cutting about Anglo Amalgamated Distributors. It seems that in advance of his meeting with Willoughby, Hargeaves and Deutsch, Collard has asked Glidrose what they made of Anglo Amalgamated. Griffie-Williams wrote that the feeling was that they were not very ambitious, and that the resulting film might be 'mediocre'. She also revealed that Rank were unwilling to sell the book's film rights, which had been sold to them outright, but that despite Willoughby's option with Rank being due to expire, the company were prepared to 'play along' with him. She added: 'On checking past correspondence, it does seem that Willoughby will make an entirely different film from the book. He does, I think, intend to create a new character which he can follow up in any subsequent film.'[36]

This was a potentially crucial point. Three years earlier, another independent producer, Kevin McClory, had provided a massive legal headache for Ian Fleming over *Thunderball*, and had won the right to remake that film (which he later did, as *Never Say Never Again*). As a result, Glidrose had sound reasons for wondering whether, were *The Diamond Smugglers* to prove a box office success, Willoughby and Todd might try to produce sequels to it featuring 'John Blaine'. And if they did, who would own the rights to this character, who was an amalgam of a real agent, John Collard, a fictionalised version of him created by Ian Fleming, and a further re-imagining by Jon Cleary, Kingsley Amis and several other writers?

WE DON'T KNOW what happened at Collard's meeting with Willoughby, Hargreaves and Deutsch, but at any rate Willoughby pressed on. On 9 February 1966, another article appeared in *The San Mateo Times*, headlined 'Newspaper Stories by Ian Fleming In Film':

> '"The Diamond Spy", an unpublished story by the late Ian Fleming, creator of James Bond, will be brought to the screen by Joseph E. Levine's Embassy Pictures in conjunction with Anglo Amalgamated Film Distributors, Ltd. of London, headed by Nat Cohen and Stuart Levy.
> The five-million dollar co-production will be produced by George Willoughby, from screenplay by W. H. Cannaway [sic] and Kingsley Amis. Director and cast for the adventure-thriller have not yet been set. "The Diamond Spy" also will be based in part on a series of newspaper articles written by Fleming and published in paper-back form under the title, "Diamond Smugglers". The story of the smashing of a huge international band of diamond racketeers, it will be filmed in color on location in South Africa, Beirut, Amsterdam, Germany and London. Embassy Pictures will distribute the film worldwide, with the exception of the United Kingdom. The last film venture involving the two companies was "Darling", which has won acclaim at both the box-office and from critics everywhere.'[37]

This was an advance on the article that had appeared in the same newspaper five months earlier. The 'James Bond' error was not repeated, although a new one was introduced – that the story was unpublished – and then contradicted. Two new locations were listed, Beirut and London, neither of which were in Cleary's script.

The next piece of news came four days later, in one of Ian Fleming's favourite newspapers, Jamaica's *Daily Gleaner*. It was titled 'Another Bond film':

> 'Of the making of James Bond films there seems to be no end. It has recently been announced that British novelist Kingsley Amis, an authority on the work of Ian Fleming, is to be special story and script consultant on "The Diamond Spy", which George Willoughby is to make in association with Richard Todd's independent company.
>
> The film will be based upon a story outline which Fleming never completed. It was drafted after his investigations for the London Sunday Times into international diamond smuggling. The series of articles he wrote were later published in book form and entitled The Diamond Smugglers. The Diamond Spy, which is scheduled to cost about £1,500,000, will be filmed almost entirely on location in South Africa, Beirut, Amsterdam, the Baltic coast of The Federal Republic of Germany and London. It has not yet been announced who will play Bond.'[38]

This is similar to the previous *San Mateo Times* piece, but Embassy and Anglo-Amalgamated have now been replaced by 'Richard Todd's independent company' and we have another reference to an uncompleted story outline by Fleming. Canaway is not mentioned: in a letter to John Collard on 19 April 1966, Willoughby explained that he had fallen ill and been replaced by Robert Muller, who had completed his first draft that week. Muller was a former theatre and film critic who had written for the prestigious *Armchair Theatre* TV series in Britain; he later married the actress Billie Whitelaw. As with the outlines by Fleming and

Amis and the work of Derry Quinn and Anthony Dawson, the whereabouts of his script are unknown.

ON 14 MARCH 1966, *Boxoffice* reported that Nat Cohen had left for New York the previous week for 'a series of production discussions' about four projected Anglo-Amalgamated films: an adaptation of *Far From The Madding Crowd*, slated to star Julie Christie; *Rocket To The Moon*, based on Jules Verne's novel; *Lock Up Your Daughters!*, the Lionel Bart musical; and *The Diamond Spy*, 'based on the Ian Fleming story'.[39] The other three films would all be produced and released within the next three years: only the Fleming project failed to make it onto celluloid.

Willoughby's letter to Collard on 19 April had contained another oddity: instead of the usual 'Willoughby Film Productions Limited' heading, the letterhead now read 'Cleon Productions Limited,' and listed the company's directors as Richard Todd and George W. Willoughby. The company was mentioned in another article in the *San Mateo Times* – evidently Willoughby's preferred outlet for his press releases – in August 1966:

'Film on Diamond Racketeers Being Made From Fleming Book

Robert Muller has been set to prepare the final screenplay of Joseph E Levine's "The Diamond Spy", the unpublished story by the late Ian Fleming, which will be bought to the screen by Levine's Embassy Pictures in conjunction with Nat Cohen's Cleon Productions Ltd.
The five-million-dollar co-production will be produced by George Willoughby, and is tentatively set to go before the color cameras late this year. The story of the smashing of a huge international band of diamond racketeers, it will be

filmed in color on location in South Africa, Beirut, Amsterdam, West Germany and London.
Embassy Pictures will distribute the film worldwide, with the exception of the United Kingdom.'[40]

So it would appear that Nat Cohen had set up a new company with Willoughby and Todd, Cleon Productions. Perhaps it was a cheeky take on Eon, with Cohen and Levine's initials added.

On June 7 1966, Willoughby wrote to Collard to invite him to a meeting at his offices with the director John Boorman, then just starting out on his career.[41] But at this point, the correspondence and the newspaper articles dry up – it seems that Willoughby had finally run out of steam. Expectations for the project had changed: from the early idea that it should not try to emulate the James Bond films but have its own flavour, as time went on, the pressure had increased to make it more Bond-like. In a letter to John Collard on June 1 1966, Willoughby had said that the film's distributors 'equate Fleming with Bond and our difficulty is to strike a story line that has all the excitement that people expect from Fleming's stories, without going into the ridiculous fantasy of the present Bond films'[42]

SHORTLY AFTER THIS, it seems the project finally petered out, and *The Diamond Smugglers* went the way of countless other film projects – although not for want of trying. Kingsley Amis returned to writing novels, and a couple of years later was commissioned to write the first post-Fleming Bond adventure, which was published as *Colonel Sun*. Bob Parrish became one of the five directors to work on Charles Feldman's Bond spoof *Casino Royale*, while John Boorman went on to direct the likes of *Point Blank*, *Deliverance* and

The Tailor of Panama. Richard Todd continued his career as an actor on stage and screen until his death from cancer in December 2009.

Jon Cleary became a best-selling thriller-writer, penning a long-running series about a Sydney cop called Scobie Malone. The first novel in the series, *The High Commissioner*, was published in 1966. Malone is charged with arresting the Australian High Commissioner in London for murder, but finds he has to stop an assassination plot against the same man by a gang of Vietnamese terrorists. The character of Malone – tough but honest, laconic but empathetic – is not a million miles from Roy O'Brien. By the end of the novel, Malone has fallen in love with a young Dutch-born Australian girl called Lisa Pretorious, herself not dissimilar to Vicki Linden; they later marry. At one point in the novel Malone lets slip to Lisa that he is a civil servant, and she asks if he has a number, 'like James Bond'.[43] The book was filmed in 1968 as *Nobody Runs Forever*, with Rod Taylor as Malone; Ralph Thomas directed.

According to Cleary, the death knell for *The Diamond Smugglers* was internal politics at Rank. 'Rank liked my script,' he says. 'But then Earl St John, who was handling the project there, fell ill. A London lawyer whose name I forget [Michael Stanley-Evans] succeeded him, and his first step was to publicly announce that he was discontinuing all projects that had been started by St John.'

Cleary remained justifiably proud of his screenplay of *The Diamond Smugglers*: as well as being a gripping story, it has the DNA of Fleming's book running through it, and is infused with both the intrigues of the diamond-smuggling business and the dramatic landscape of South Africa. It remains a fascinating what-if in cinema history, as we are left to wonder what impact it might have had if George Willoughby had succeeded in bringing it to cinema screens in the Sixties, and John Blaine had battled it out with James Bond at the box office.

Notes for this chapter:

1. *The Letters of Kingsley Amis*, edited by Zachary Leader (HarperCollins, 2001), pp664-665.
2. *In Camera: An Autobiography Continued* by Richard Todd (Hutchinson, 1989), p196.
3. *United Artists: The Company that Changed the Film Industry* by Tino Balio (University of Wisconsin Press, 1987), p257.
4. *In Camera* by Todd, p205.
5. Personal correspondence with Fergus Fleming, January 27 2010.
6. *Ian Fleming* by Andrew Lycett (Phoenix, 1996), p258.
7. Obituary of John Collard, *The Times*, 13 November 2002.
8. Lycett, p310.
9. 'Memorandum on diamond-buying operations in Liberia, April/May 1955', annotated by Ian Fleming, in John Collard's papers. John Collard's book, correspondence and other papers, all courtesy of Paul Collard and the Collard family. Henceforth Collard Papers.
10. *James Bond: The Man and His World* by Henry Chancellor (John Murray, 2005), p113.
11. *The Diamond Smugglers* by Ian Fleming (Pan, 1965 edition), p150.
12. Collard to Russell, handwritten letter, December 30 1965, Collard Papers.
13. Lycett, p316.
14. Chancellor, p85.
15. 'The Ian Fleming Collection of 19th-20th Century Source Material Concerning Western Civilization together with the Originals of the James Bond-007 Tales', Lilly Library, Indiana University, Bloomington, United States.
16. Lycett, p264.

17. *The Bookseller*, Compendium of Issues 2698-2714 (Publishers' Association, Booksellers Association of Great Britain and Ireland, 1957), p1808.
18. *In Camera*, p187.
19. Ibid., p215.
20. Ibid., p237.
21. This and all subsequent Jon Cleary quotes from a telephone conversation with the author, November 30 2007.
22. *The Ageless Land: The Story of South-West Africa* by Olga Levinson (Tafelberg, 1961).
23. This and all subsequent quotes from *The Diamond Smugglers* screenplay by Jon Cleary courtesy of Jon Cleary; Curtis Brown, London; and the Mitchell Library, the State Library of New South Wales, Australia.
24. Letter from George Willoughby to John Collard, June 14 1965. Collard Papers.
25. Letter from John Collard to George Willoughby, June 17 1965. Collard Papers.
26. Letter from George Willoughby to John Collard, June 21 1965. Collard Papers.
27. Letter from B.J. Rudd to John Collard, September 1 1965, with cutting from *The Sun* attached. Collard Papers. According to Andrew Lycett, Ian Fleming had told Rank at the time they had taken the option on *The Diamond Smugglers* that he would provide them with a 'full story outline' for a further £1,000, but would not be able to bind himself to writing 'the master scene script' or to be available in England for consultations. Lycett, p317.
28. Letter from George Willoughby to John Collard, August 27 1965. Collard Papers.
29. Personal correspondence with Anthony Dawson Jr, 2007-2009.
30. 'The Marquee column', Barbara Bladen, September 16 1965, *San Mateo Times*, p21.
31. Letter from John Collard to George Willoughby, January 3 1966. Collard Papers.
32. Letter from George Willoughby to John Collard, January 11 1966. Collard Papers.

33 Anthony Gruner, 'London Report', *Boxoffice*, January 3 1966. The same column also announced that Ursula Andress and David Niven were to join Peter Sellers in the cast of Charles Feldman's *Casino Royale*.

34. Anthony Gruner, 'London Report', *Boxoffice*, November 29, 1965.

35. Letter from George Willoughby to John Collard, January 27, 1966. Collard Papers.

36. Letter from Beryl Griffie-Williams to John Collard, January 31, 1966. Collard Papers.

37. *San Mateo Times*, California, February 9, 1966. An almost identically worded paragraph appeared in Anthony Gruner's 'London Report' column in *Boxoffice* on 7 February 1966.

38. *The Gleaner*, Jamaica, February 13, 1966.

39. Anthony Gruner, 'London Report', *Boxoffice*, March 14, 1966.

40. *San Mateo Times*, California, August 26, 1966.

41. Letter from George Willoughby to John Collard, June 7, 1966. Collard Papers.

42. Letter from George Willoughby to John Collard, June 1, 1966. Collard Papers.

43. *The High Commissioner* by Jon Cleary (Fontana, 1983 edition), p62.

Commando Bond

'MI6 LOOKS FOR maladjusted young men who'd give little thought to sacrificing others to protect queen and country. You know – former SAS types with easy smiles and expensive watches…'

So says Vesper Lynd to James Bond in the 2006 film *Casino Royale*. Although it doesn't get as much mileage in the finished film as it did in the press before its release, *Casino Royale* took a daring approach to the Bond mythos, presenting an 'origin story' for the character. Bond is a newly appointed member of MI6's Double O Section – the film opens with him earning his stripes by cold-bloodedly murdering a traitor – and it would appear from his reaction to Vesper's comment that she has hit home and that he is in fact a 'former SAS type'. This was confirmed by the film's official website, which provided a chronology of Bond's pre-MI6 career, including a military dossier detailing his time at Britannia Royal Naval College, his intelligence role on HMS

Exeter and special forces training at Plymouth and Brize Norton. The site even claimed Bond had been part of an invented outfit called '030 Special Forces Unit'.[1]

Special forces have developed a particular image in popular culture in recent years. Britain's SAS is probably the world's best known special forces outfit, having featured in dozens of films, books and magazine articles, many of them generated by the worldwide media interest surrounding the storming of the Iranian Embassy in London in 1980 after terrorists took hostages inside, which was screened live on British television.

Members of the SAS have a popular image as gung-ho operators who shoot first and ask questions later: not really the type to create their own cocktails (or sport easy smiles). The use of tough SAS types in fiction has also become something of a cliché, with a whole genre being formed in the wake of Andy McNab's 1993 memoir of an SAS operation in Iraq, *Bravo Two Zero*. It's not quite James Bond territory. Or...?

In an article in TIME published shortly before the release of *Die Another Day*, Lee Tamahori, the director of that film, made the following remark about the direction he felt the character had been taken in the previous few films:

> "'I was worried that he was turning into an SAS man, machine-gunning everyone," says Tamahori. "I've been trying to make him more of an Ian Fleming Bond.'"[2]

This is a misapprehension. While copious use of a machine gun is not a hallmark of Ian Fleming's novels, the idea that James Bond might be an SAS man is not out of keeping with them. In fact, Fleming included several clues that point to James Bond having just such a type of background.

The Special Air Service didn't always have the popular reputation it has today. The group was founded by David

Stirling in 1941 to undertake acts of sabotage behind enemy lines. The son of a Scottish general, Stirling began a degree in architecture at Trinity College, Cambridge, but his studies were curtailed by his fondness for the local nightlife. He was eventually read out a list of 23 offences and asked to choose the three for which he wished to be sent down. He then decided to become the first man to climb Everest and enlisted in the Supplementary Reserves of the Scots Guards – he trained in the Swiss Alps and the Rockies. When war broke out he was 24, and was sent to the Guards Depot in Pirbright:

> 'Pirbright was a mere hour from the attractions of London. During one lecture, possibly after a night at White's Club or the gaming tables, Stirling fell asleep. He probably fell asleep in many, but on this occasion he was woken by the lecturer, asking him to repeat what had just been said. Stirling repeated it verbatim.'[3]

After this, Stirling volunteered for an expeditionary force setting off to fight a winter campaign in Finland – ski training was in Chamonix – before joining the commando group Layforce, after which he founded the SAS.

It's hard to imagine a more 'James Bondish' background than this, but Stirling is one of the few leading commandos from the Second World War not to have been claimed as a model for 007. Fleming was certainly inspired by the real-life experience of such men, however, as he made clear in an interview with Playboy published after his death:

> 'I think [Bond is] slightly more true to the type of modern hero, to the commandos of the last War, and so on, and to some of the secret-service men I've met, than to any of the rather cardboardy heroes of the ancient thrillers.'[4]

Fleming knew several heroic commandos and secret-service men who had served in the war. Perhaps the best known among them is Patrick Leigh Fermor, who worked for the Special Operations Executive (SOE) in Crete, where he led the party that kidnapped General Kreipe in 1944. That mission was immortalised in W Stanley Moss' book *Ill Met By Moonlight*, published in 1950, which was made into a film in 1957, with Dirk Bogarde playing Leigh Fermor.

In an afterword for the 2001 edition of Moss' book, Leigh Fermor wrote about the operation for the first time. He modestly refuted the 'Baroness Orczy - John Buchan - Dornford Yates' status that the episode has gained over the years, but at the same time revealed that during a prolonged stay in Cairo with SOE colleagues, the villa they had stayed in had been filled with gelignite disguised as goat's droppings, magnetised trouser buttons that turned into compasses and gossamer-thin maps stitched into the lining of clothing. Many of these items were created by a Major Jasper Maskelyne, who Leigh Fermor recognised as a stage magician he had seen perform in London as a child.[5]

After the war, Leigh Fermor took up writing, drafting some of his first book, *The Traveller's Tree*, during a stay at Goldeneye in 1948. He loved Fleming's Jamaican retreat and commented in his book that it could become a model for new houses in the tropics.[6] The two men became friends, and Fleming repaid Fermor's plug for Goldeneye by quoting a long passage on voodoo from *The Traveller's Tree* in *Live and Let Die*.

Another of Fleming's friends mentioned in his novels was David Niven, whose manners Kissy Suzuki so admires that she names her cormorant after him. Niven also served as a commando of sorts in the Second World War: while serving with 'Phantom', the regiment responsible for ferreting out information in forward areas and radioing it back to GHQ, he worked on joint operations with the SAS, whose command it came under from 1944.[7]

Another friend, Anthony Terry, was captured during Operation CHARIOT, the daring commando raid on the harbour installations at Saint-Nazaire in 1942, and was awarded the Military Cross for it.[8] After the war, he worked for Fleming's Mercury News, as well as continuing his contacts with MI6, and in 1960, he guided Fleming around Berlin, helping him with much of the research for the short story *The Living Daylights*.[9]

Closer to home, Ian Fleming's brother Peter was also engaged in commando work during the war. In 1940, he and 'Mad Mike' Calvert – who later found fame with the SAS – prepared for a guerrilla defence of Britain the event of a German invasion. Later that year, Peter Fleming led a reconnaissance party into the Norwegian port of Namsos and the following year he formed and took a small commando team to Greece (the latter mission under the auspices of SOE). Neither expedition was a great success: Peter was reported to have been killed in Norway and an obituary even ran in *The Daily Sketch*, causing his family great distress until he arrived, alive and well, in Scotland. It may be that this episode later gave Ian the idea for Bond's false obituary in *You Only Live Twice*: it can be useful for a secret agent to have the world believe him dead.

In Greece, the Yak Mission, as Peter's group was nicknamed, wrecked the path of advancing German paratroops – Peter even booby-trapped a bridge by fitting a London double-decker bus with flame-throwers on it – before it was attacked from the air near the island of Milos. A

400-ton yacht that had been commandeered by the Navy burst into flames and sank, and Peter was again very lucky to come out alive.[10]

Peter Fleming was also a celebrated travel writer and journalist. His novel *The Sixth Column*, published in 1951, was a gentle send-up of the thrillers he had enjoyed growing up, and was dedicated to Ian, also an aficionado of the genre. One of the main characters is a former commando called Archie Strume, who has great success with a thriller based on his war-time experiences titled 'Hackforth of The Commandos'. Colonel Hackforth is always saying things like:

> 'Tell the Minister of Defence to have a midget submarine alongside the Harwich customs jetty not later than last light on Tuesday. It's important.'[11]

The Sixth Column may have been a spur for Ian Fleming to knuckle down and write his own thriller, which he had been promising to do since the war: he started writing *Casino Royale* just a few months after the publication of his brother's book. Archie Strume and Colonel Hackforth were partially based on the author Dennis Wheatley – who Peter had become friends with during the war – and his secret agent character Gregory Sallust, but the references to wartime commando adventures involving midget submarines may have been for Ian's eyes only,

In 1942, Ian Fleming set up what he liked to call his 'Red Indians'. No. 30 Assault Unit was a small roving commando outfit made up of men from the Army, Navy, Marines and Air Force. Its task was to go in after the first wave of Allied attacks and scavenge for technical intelligence: codes, weapons, equipment, maps and documents left behind by the Germans. The commanding officers were Dunstan Curtis, who had played a leading role in the Saint Nazaire raid, and the Antarctic explorer Quentin Riley.[12]

One of 30 AU's most enterprising officers was Lieutenant-Commander Patrick Dalzel-Job RNVR, who led missions in France, Belgium and Germany in the latter stages of the war. Dalzel-Job had an unusual background: after the death of his father in the Somme, he spent his formative years in Switzerland, where he learned to cross-country ski and speak French fluently. While still in his twenties, he built his own schooner and sailed to Norway with his middle-aged mother and a Norwegian schoolgirl as his crew.

This experience stood him in good stead when the war came. In April 1940, when Peter Fleming was in Namsos, Dalzel-Job was in Narvik, where he countermanded orders not to evacuate civilians. Later on, he worked behind the scenes developing the Royal Navy's midget submarines, used in the attack on the Tirpitz, and finally went behind enemy lines with 30 AU, where among other things, he accepted the formal surrender of the city of Bremen and captured the Nazis' own midget submarines.

Dalzel-Job did not care overly for his boss back in London, finding Ian Fleming cold, austere and egotistical, although he appreciated his 'amusing and pungent' minutes on operational intelligence reports.[13] Dalzel-Job's 'Nelson touch' even brought him into conflict with Fleming at the end of the war, when he sent a signal to the British Flag Officer in Oslo as though it were from the Admiralty, sending himself on a fairly pointless mission to Norway so he could find the schoolgirl he had sailed with before the war. Fleming was furious at not being consulted, and gave Dalzel-Job an earful about it, but off he went, found the girl, and married her.

Another member of 30 AU who saw action in France was Tony Hugill. Also a lieutenant-commander in the Royal Naval Volunteer Reserve , he was awarded the Croix de Guerre for his part in D-Day and won the Distinguished Service Cross for taking the surrender of 280 troops under a Luftwaffe officer at a radio station near Brest. From 1945-6, he led the Forward Interrogation Unit in Hamburg, Germany.

After the war, Hugill went into the sugar industry, managing Tate and Lyle's West Indian operations between 1954 and 1966. In Fleming's last novel, *The Man With The Golden Gun*, Bond is vouched for by local sugar executive Tony Hugill, who, we learn in Chapter 4, was in Naval Intelligence during the war: 'sort of Commando job'. Bond's cover name for this mission, Mark Hazard, may have been inspired by the title of Hugill's war memoirs, *The Hazard Mesh*, published in 1946, but if so Fleming either hadn't read the book or was in a generous mood, because Hugill's depiction of him (although he is not named) is not flattering:

> 'One of the Admiralty pundits signalled us that he was about to honour us with a visit. We none of us liked him much. He was one of those very superior professorial type R.N.V.R.s who got their claws into Their Lordships early in the war and have kept them in ever since. As our proprietary deity he felt himself entitled to demand offerings of Camembert and libations of captured cognac of the better sort (But my dear feller this stuff's undrinkable!) from time to time. He also interfered with us on a higher level.'[14]

After Fleming's death, Hugill described Fleming in gentler terms.[15] In contrast to the popular perception of commandos today, the British commandos Fleming knew from the war were often, beneath their tough exteriors, cultured men of great sensitivity: Patrick Leigh-Fermor and Peter Fleming were both acclaimed travel writers, Tony Hugill's memoirs are filled with poetry and Patrick Dalzel-Job's autobiography is, at root, a love story.

Fleming never saw action in the field himself, although he may have liked to have done. John Pearson recounted in his biography that Fleming liked to tell people, Gatsby-ishly, that he had once killed a man, but that the story seemed to change with each telling[16], and some of his other claims of prowess have been similarly questioned.

This sense of inconsistency extended to James Bond. In his fiction, Fleming made use of those real-life episodes he found most fascinating and exciting; ensuring that all of his novels' re-imagined tidbits meshed together was of secondary concern. For example, Fleming fans the world over know that James Bond killed twice in cold blood to obtain his licence to kill – nobody cares to dwell on the irritatingly inconvenient sentence in Chapter 19 of *From Russia, With Love* in which Fleming baldly states 'Bond had never killed in cold blood.'

THE TWO KILLINGS described in *Casino Royale* are both examples of operations usually undertaken by special forces: assassinations. Governments and conventional intelligence services cannot be seen to sanction extra-judicial murder, so such jobs inevitably fall to less accountable units. As Bond's second kill, in Stockholm, involved a Norwegian 'who was doubling against us for the Germans', it appears that both these missions took place during the war. According to MRD Foot's official history of the SOE, Stockholm had been the initial base for that organisation's activity in Scandinavia[17], so perhaps Fleming had heard of a similar operation through intelligence contacts and embellished it.[18]

Bond's first 'wet job', in New York's Rockefeller Center, was inspired by Fleming's visit to the British Security Co-ordination's offices in the same building in June 1941; he accompanied BSC officers as they burgled a Japanese cipher clerk's office on the floor below theirs.[19] The clerk was unharmed, but SOE, whose affairs in the Western hemisphere were controlled by the BSC in New York[20], did have an assassination capability. This was officially abandoned at the end of the war, but many SOE officers joined MI6, so the expertise may have remained in place[21]. During the war, SOE operatives were commonly referred to as 'terrorists' by the Nazis; MRD Foot, who was a member of SAS during the war, recalls being captured and over-hearing one of his interrogators saying: 'If he is a terrorist he is shot at once'.[22]

After the war, the SAS evolved into more of a counter-insurgency regiment; the 1969 Army Training manual stated that its tasks included 'the ambush and harassment of insurgents, the infiltration of sabotage, assassination and demolition parties into insurgent-held areas, border surveillance liaison with, and organisation of friendly guerrilla forces operating against the common enemy'.[23] The SAS executed some of these responsibilities in the Mau-Mau rebellion in Kenya during the 1950s and in Aden in 1967.[24] More recently, it has seen action in Aghanistan, Northern Ireland, Gibraltar and, latterly, Iraq.

Despite the above rather lurid description, members of the SAS have not always approved of assassination. When I asked former SAS sergeant Jacques Goffinet in 2005 if he had been tempted to assassinate Joachim von Ribbentrop when he discovered him in hiding in a flat in Hamburg in June 1945, he replied simply: 'That would have made me as bad as them.'[25]

James Bond is often concerned with the same dilemma: outside of the episodes mentioned in *Casino Royale*, he makes for a rather shaky assassin. In the short story *Octopussy*, he travels to Jamaica on a private war crimes investigation. His target is Dexter Smythe, who as a member of the Miscellaneous Objectives Bureau – a (fictional) wartime commando outfit formed by the Secret Service and Combined Operations – had murdered one of his early mentors. But while Bond had no qualms about murdering double agents or cipher clerks, this time he does not draw his weapon, leaving Smythe the options of suicide or disgrace.

In *The Living Daylights*, Bond's mission is strategically defensive – to stop another assassination – but here he also has reservations, and deliberately muffs the assignment because of the 'sharp pang of longing' he feels for his female target – a sackable offence, as he admits himself at the end of the story. In *For Your Eyes Only*, Bond undertakes the mission to assassinate Von Hammerstein as retribution for the murder of M's friends: an 'eye for an eye job'. In the event, however, the deed is done by the friends' daughter, although Bond kills another of the villains and comforts the girl afterwards. In *The Man With The Golden Gun*, Bond is a little less circumspect, eventually shooting Scaramanga five times.

JAMES BOND IS neither straightforward assassin nor pure commando in Ian Fleming's novels: most of the time he works as a counter-espionage agent, sent by M to head off an emerging threat, rather than initiating offensive action against the enemy. Nevertheless, Fleming incorporated many details of war-time commandos into his novels: apart from the references to old colleagues and friends who had been involved in special forces, Q Branch's weapons and gadgets parallel the work done by similar departments in SOE and elsewhere. Bond's self-reliance and stamina are reminiscent of the commando ethic, as is his basic fitness regimen described in Chapter 11 of *From Russia, With Love*. His habit of taking Benzedrine was also common practice among commandos during the war, when remaining alert for long periods was often necessary.

Bond is also a martial arts aficionado – we know from M's obituary in *You Only Live Twice* that he founded the first judo class in a British public school. In Chapter 10 of the same novel, Tiger Tanaka tells Bond he will show him one of his service's secret ninja academies in the mountains, and Bond replies that MI6 also has a commando training school for unarmed combat attached to its headquarters. This is an example of Fleming carrying details across his books successfully, because in Chapter 8 of *Moonraker* Bond is happy to have his Unarmed Combat class with 'that dam' Commando chap' cancelled for a meeting with M. Bond is clearly a good student, though, because in the first chapter of *Goldfinger* we find him nursing the hand that has killed a Mexican with a 'Parry Defence against Underhand Thrust out of the book' and a hand-edge blow to the Adam's Apple that had been 'the standby of the Commandos'. A little later, in Chapter 5, we learn that Bond is writing *Stay Alive!*, a 'handbook of all methods of unarmed combat'.

But Bond also uses weapons, of course. In Chapter 18 of *Live and Let Die*, he tries to kill an octopus using a commando dagger 'of the type devised by Wilkinson's during the war'. This would be the Fairbairn-Sykes Fighting Knife, issued to the SAS and other special forces outfits and eventually adopted as the Commando Association's emblem. It's still made by Wilkinson's, still in use by British special forces[26] and is currently the shoulder-flash of the Royal Marine Commandos.[27]

The idea that this character has had some sort of experience with special forces is not implausible – but what form might that have taken? In *The James Bond Dossier*, Kingsley Amis wondered what a Commander from Naval Intelligence had been doing in the Ardennes sector in 1944[28] (which Bond recollects in Chapter Nine of *Dr No*). This may simply have been an oversight on Fleming's part, like the 'cold blood' boo-boo in *From Russia, With Love*, but it may also have been deliberate. In his obituary in *You Only Live Twice*, M tells us that Bond joined the Special Branch of the RNVR in 1941. Between that date and 1944, Peter Fleming undertook missions for both MI R and SOE; army intelligence officer Anthony Terry was captured in a naval commando raid; RAF men took part in 30 AU's amphibious landings with Royal Naval Commandos; and Patrick Leigh Fermor and SOE colleagues arranged for guides to help Special Boat Service (SBS) officers across the mountains of Crete.[29] The Second World War was a time of irregular warfare, and resourceful young men barging into offices in Whitehall demanding to mount their own raids against the Nazis were not uncommon. Dozens of small commando units were formed, changed names or were subsumed into larger groups during the war, and as a result some enterprising men had extremely varied resumes by the cessation of hostilities. Churchill also set up Combined Operations under Lord Mountbatten, which ensured that commando groups worked together (like Dexter Smythe's outfit in *Octopussy*). For Operation

FRANKTON, for example, a raid on Bordeaux Harbour in December 1942, the Royal Marine Boom Patrol's Detachment used limpet mines that had been developed by SOE[30] – or 'those things our saboteurs used against ships in the war', as Bond describes them in Chapter 15 of *Live and Let Die* (later in the book he attaches a limpet mine to the hull of the Secatur).

Against this background, it's not so unlikely for someone in the Special Branch of the RNVR to have heard machine-gun fire in the Ardennes. Unless Fleming meant for Bond to have been an infantry soldier at the Battle of the Bulge – which seems even more unlikely for someone in the RNVR – by far the most likely way for him to have been in the area would have been on a special forces mission. SOE's Operation CITRONELLE, which sought out *maquis* in the Ardennes in April 1944, for example: he could have been a member of one of the famous Jedburgh teams, all of which contained one Brit, one American and one Frenchman – early training for working with Felix Leiter and René Mathis, perhaps. SOE produced more than its fair share of successes during the war: one of its best-known agents was the Polish-born countess Krystyna Skarbek, best known as Christine Granville.[33]

Another plausible explanation is that Bond was seconded to the SAS: it drew and still draws men from all armed forces (the 'Air' in its name was used to fit in with an earlier deception operation), and undertook several missions in the Ardennes during 1944.[34] Fleming might easily have heard about one of these operations from David Niven or another friend who had worked with the regiment, and stored it away as being a suitable field of operation for Bond during the war.

Most obviously, perhaps, Fleming's own brainchild, 30 Assault Unit, also undertook reconnaissance work in Belgium at around this time, and in his 2013 novel *Solo* William Boyd has Bond remember this episode and suggests he was attached to that unit. Boyd wasn't the first author after Fleming to emphasise 007's special forces ties: John Gardner – who served in the Royal Marines' 42 Commando during the war – had Bond train with the SAS and the SBS in his novels.[35] The relationship has been even more overt onscreen: the closing scenes of many of the films, for example, are spectacular commando-like raids on villains' lairs. HALO jumps, bungee jumps, parachute landings and shooting while skiing are all areas of special forces expertise. The recent Bond films continue the series' habitual nods to special forces work: in *Casino Royale*, as well as Vesper's appraisal, Bond holds up an embassy single-handedly and engages in plenty of hand-to-hand combat – he seems to have paid attention in his classes with that dam' Commando.

The Bond novels and films have never purported to be realistic portrayals of clandestine work: they are fantastic adventures with one toe in the real world. James Bond is an amalgamation and elaboration of the most exciting bits of espionage and commando lore, filtered through the prodigious imagination of his creator. He is not, therefore, an out and out commando, but as a back story for the character, 'former SAS type' is not out of place: it is entirely fitting with his heritage. And, as I'll explore in the next chapter, some of the special forces history that inspired Fleming would also inspire the Bond film-makers.

Notes for this chapter:

1. Now archived, but accessed December 20 2014 from: https://web.archive.org/web/20061129205105/http://www.sonypictures.com/movies/casinoroyale/site_html/dossier/military_record.php
2. *TIME*, November 10 2002.
3. *The Originals: The Secret History of The Birth of the SAS In Their Own Words* by Gordon Stevens (Ebury Press, 2005), p4.
4.. *The Playboy Interview: Ian Fleming* by Ken Purdy, *Playboy*, December 1964.
5.. *Ill Met By Moonlight* by W Stanley Moss, The Folio Society, 2001: afterword by Leigh Fermor, pp193 and 205-206.
6. *The Traveller's Tree* by Patrick Leigh Fermor, Penguin, 1984, p327.
7. *The SAS: The Official History* by Philip Warner (Sphere, 1983), p139; and obituary of Captain Charles Moore, *The Daily Telegraph*, May 13 2004.
8. *The Greatest Raid Of All* by CE Lucas-Phillips (Little, Brown, 1960), pix.
9. *Ian Fleming* by Andrew Lycett (Phoenix, 1996), p371.
10. *Peter Fleming: A Biography* by Duff Hart Davis (Oxford University Press, 1987), pp221-227 and 239-255.
11. *The Sixth Column* by Peter Fleming (Tandem, 1967), p23.
12. *The Life of Ian Fleming* by John Pearson (Companion Book Club, 1966), p134.
13. *Arctic Snow to Dust of Normandy: The Extraordinary Wartime Exploits of a Naval Special Agent* by Patrick Dalzel-Job (Pen & Sword, 2005), p115.
14. p60 *The Hazard Mesh* by JAC Hugill, Hurst & Blackett, 1946.
15. *Ian Fleming's Commandos* by Nicholas Rankin (Faber & Faber, 2011), pp247-48.
16. p210 Pearson.
17. p208 *SOE: 1940-1946* by MRD Foot, BBC, 1984
18. As well as his colleagues in Naval Intelligence, Fleming crossed paths with many people involved in clandestine work during the war.
19. p124 Pearson
20. p42 Foot
21. pp 611-612 *MI6: Inside the Covert World of Her Majesty's Secret Intelligence Service* by Stephen Dorril, Touchstone, 2000

22. p57 Foot. James Bond is also described as a terrorist, in his MGB file in Chapter Six of *From Russia, With Love*. Incidentally, Foot feels that Fleming was one of the few non-SOE officers in Britain's wartime intelligence organisations to appreciate SOE's worth (personal communication, November 17 2007)

23. British Army Land Operations Manual, volume 3, counter-revolutionary operations. Cited in *British Intelligence and Covert Action* by Jonathan Bloch and Pat Fitzgerald (London 1982), p42.

24. 'The SAS, their early days in Ireland and the Wilson Plot', Alexander Platow (Seán Mac Mathúna), first published in *Lobster* 18 (1989).

25. See *Whisper Who Dares* by Jeremy Duns, June 16 2005, *The Bulletin*, Brussels; reprinted in *5 SAS' Veterans' News*, Issue 70, 2005.

26. p389 *Jane's Special Forces Recognition Guide* by Ewen Southby-Tailyour, Collins, 2005

27. p47 *British Commandos 1940-1946* by Tim Moreman, Osprey, 2006

28. p17 *The James Bond Dossier* by Kingsley Amis, Signet, 1966

29. p194 Leigh Fermor afterword, Moss

30 *Cockleshell Heroes* by CE Lucas-Phillips (Pan, 1974), p36. FRANKTON was masterminded by Herbert 'Blondie' Hasler, who went on to play a leading role in the founding of the Special Boat Service (SBS), a sister service to the SAS. The operation was the subject of the 1955 film *The Cockleshell Heroes*, produced by Cubby Broccoli and co-written by Richard Maibaum.

31. Granville has been repeatedly claimed to have been Fleming's model for Vesper Lynd following a post-war affair with the author. The source for this appears to be p151 *17F: The Life of Ian Fleming* by Donald McCormick, Peter Owen, London, 1993. McCormick is known to have been a hoaxer, notably on matters related to Jack the Ripper, and I believe he fabricated the evidence for this plausible-sounding assumption. Regardless, there seem very few similarities between Granville and Vesper Lynd other than their both being beautiful female agents with dark hair.

32. Ewen Southby-Tailyour does not agree with me on this point, being adamant that Fleming's Bond would have been more likely to have been SBS than SAS. He points to Bond's naval background and

the fact that every member of the SBS was trained in skiing, parachuting, mountaineering and combat (underwater) swimming – but very few members of the SAS undertook training in all of these (personal communication). However, the SAS often collaborated and exchanged personnel with naval units during the war, and the SBS never undertook any operations in the Ardennes.

33. See, for instance, p15, *Icebreaker* by John Gardner, Berkley, 1983; and p28 *Scorpius* by John Gardner, Charter, 1990

Black Tie Spy

IT'S ONE OF the most iconic – and coolest – scenes in modern cinema. A secret agent emerges from water at night wearing a wetsuit, creeps onto a heavily guarded wharf, knocks out a sentry, and plants some plastic explosive in a storage tank. He then unzips his wetsuit to reveal that he is wearing a dinner jacket beneath it, complete with a carnation in the buttonhole. He walks into the nearest bar, glances at his watch and lights a cigarette just as the storage tank erupts into flames behind him.

This, of course, is the opening scene of the third James Bond film, *Goldfinger*. Released in 1964, it turned Bond into a global phenomenon, and 007 peeling away his wetsuit to reveal black tie has become one of the most recognisable moments of the series. No such scene featured in Ian Fleming's novel of the same title, but in many ways it defines the character of James Bond: one moment a tough secret agent focused on a dangerous mission, the next a high-living playboy. It's pure fantasy, of course, and light years away from the world of real espionage.

Or perhaps not. Surprisingly enough, it seems that the scene may have been inspired by an extraordinary mission undertaken by British intelligence during the Second World War.

The operation was planned in the autumn of 1941, in a small flat above 77 Chester Square, the London residence of the exiled Dutch queen, Wilhelmina. Three young Dutchmen – Bob van der Stok, Peter Tazelaar and Erik

Hazelhoff Roelfzema – had an idea for a method of inserting an agent into occupied Holland, from which they had recently escaped.[1]

As students, the Dutchmen had often spent time at the seaside resort of Scheveningen, near The Hague. They knew that the Palace Hotel there had been taken over by the Germans as a headquarters for their coastal defence forces, and that every Friday night they held a large and boisterous party there. Their idea was both ingenious and audacious – approach Scheveningen in darkness by boat, and then take Peter Tazelaar into the surf by dinghy. He would strip off his watertight suit into evening clothes and make his way ashore, right under the noses of the Germans. If stopped by sentries, he would drunkenly claim to be one of the party-goers. From there, he would continue his mission.

Dutch intelligence in London was mired in political intriguing, and not interested in running the operation – but the British were. They were initially sceptical of the method of inserting Tazelaar onto the beach, which sounded more like a student prank than a serious proposal for an espionage operation, but the head of MI6's Dutch section, Colonel Euan Rabagliati – nicknamed 'The Rabbi' by the Dutch – eventually agreed to the plan.

The mission's aims were twofold: first, Tazelaar was to make contact with a Dutch wireless operator at a safe house and begin transmissions with London at pre-arranged times; secondly, he was to set up a wider intelligence-gathering network to provide reports, maps, photographs and other items that couldn't be transmitted over the wireless but that would be picked up by sea and taken back to London by Motor Gun Boat (ie the same way he had come). In the latter category were also two people, Dr Wiardi Beckman and a

Captain Tielens, both of whom Queen Wilhelmina wanted to join the Dutch government-in-exile in London.

TO PREPARE FOR the operation, The Rabbi sent Hazelhoff Roelfzema and Tazelaar to train at various secret establishments. They learned to shoot at a pistol range beneath Baker Street Underground station and practised boat landings off the coasts of Cornwall and Devon. An experimental watertight suit was made for Tazelaar and, so that his contacts would be in no doubt of his credentials, Queen Wilhelmina was persuaded to write a note in her own hand verifying his mission. MI6 reduced her message to the size of a fingernail, and it was placed inside the collar of Tazelaar's dress shirt.

The operation itself proved harder to pull off than anticipated, due to poor weather and the difficulties of locating Scheveningen's promenade in the dark. But after several frustrating false starts, at just after half past four in the morning on November 23 1941, Hazelhoff Roelfzema, Tazelaar and another Dutchman, Chris Krediet, along with Lieutenant Bob Goodfellow, disembarked from British Royal Navy Motor Gun Boat 321 onto a small dinghy. The Dutchmen slipped out of the dinghy as they neared the surf, and Hazelhoff Roelfzema and Tazelaar waded onto Scheveningen's beach. Hazelhoff Roelfzema helped Tazelaar unzip his watertight suit: beneath it he was wearing immaculate evening clothes. Hazelhoff Roelfzema poured a generous dose of Hennessy XO (Tazelaar's favourite) from a hip flask over his friend, and returned to the dinghy.

Now reeking of brandy, Tazelaar proceeded to stagger convincingly past the sentries stationed around the hotel.

Against all odds, the first part of his operation had succeeded. He made contact with the wireless operator, and within three days had also made contact with Dr Beckman and Captain Tielens. Then things started to go wrong. Tielens didn't want to make the journey to London, and couldn't be persuaded, but Beckman agreed to the plan. However, the return rendez-vous was beset by problems: the Motor Gun Boat didn't navigate to the meeting point on time, and then a collaborator betrayed the fact that landings were taking place at the beach to the Germans.

On January 18 1942, Hazelhoff Roelfzema arrived on the beach at a prearranged time to deliver two vitally needed transmitters to Tazelaar. But his friend was not there. Thinking quickly, he decided to bury the transmitters in the sand, to be picked up later. But how to let Tazelaar know where to find them? He knew from his student days that there was a telephone booth near the hotel. If he could reach a member of the Resistance, they could tell Tazelaar where the transmitters were buried.

Borrowing a British naval uniform from the motor gunboat, which he hoped in the darkness would resemble a German one closely enough, Hazelhoff Roelfzema embarked on his own Bond-like mission. Once ashore, he safely passed several sentries and managed to reach the telephone, where he discovered to his horror that it no longer accepted the old Dutch coins he had brought with him. Frustrated, he beat a hasty retreat to the motor gunboat, and headed back to England.

Unknown to him, Tazelaar had had a very good reason for not making the rendez-vous – he and a member of the Resistance had been picked up by the Germans while walking down to the meeting point. Amazingly, they managed to bluff their way out of it: both were wearing dinner clothes, and stuck to the cover story of being drunken revellers. Tazelaar had even brought along a bottle of genever, which he generously passed around. A local policeman, luckily also a member of the Resistance, vouched for the pair, and the Germans let them go. Dr Beckman was not as lucky: he was arrested on the beach waiting to be picked up by motor gunboat, and later died in Dachau.

THE IDEA OF landing a secret agent on an enemy coastline in a watertight suit, only for him to strip it off to reveal full evening dress and mingle with the local nightlife festivities is an exceptionally unusual one – so much so one would think it must be unique. But it is also, of course, remarkably similar to the opening sequence of the film *Goldfinger*.

The director of *Goldfinger*, Guy Hamilton, was an officer in the Royal Navy's 15th Motor Gunboat Flotilla during the war, and was involved in landing MI6 agents onto coastlines in much the same way as was done with Peter Tazelaar. But, now 87 and living in Mallorca, Hamilton says he has never heard of the operation in Holland. 'I was indeed inserting agents into enemy territory from motor gunboats during the war, but they were always as farmers or something along those lines, to blend in with the locals – never in black tie!'[2]

So if Hamilton wasn't the scene's instigator, how *did* the idea behind this remarkable wartime operation make it into *Goldfinger*? The operation wasn't public knowledge when the film was made, but it was a *cause célèbre* within British intelligence circles. According to M.R.D. Foot's official history of the Special Operations Executive (SOE), published in 1984, MI6 pulled off this operation 'in a style SOE envied'.[3]

The answer might have been hiding in plain sight. The scene in *Goldfinger* was written by a former member of SOE, Paul Dehn, who had been brought in to polish the first draft of the screenplay by Richard Maibaum. Dehn recalled how he had got the job in a 1972 interview:

> 'For twenty-five years, I was a critic in Fleet Street, working for the old *News Chronicle*, and originally when I was a critic I started writing manuscripts because I found it so hard to allocate praise and blame justly in a composite work of art like a film. The first one I wrote, in collaboration with Jimmy [James Bernard, Hammer Film composer and Dehn's professional and personal partner], was called *Seven Days To Noon*, and for which we both received an Oscar, and we also received 485 pounds from the dear Boulting brothers. So, after the Oscar film, I thought we would be rushing around writing for everybody, but two years went by and we did nothing at all. During the war I was an instructor to a band of thugs called the S.O.E. (Special Operations Executive, to which Christopher Lee was also attached for some time [as were Xan Fielding and Pierre Boulle]), and I instructed them in various things on darkened estates, so I got a pretty good view of what counter espionage was like, as a result of which, when I joined the *Daily Herald*, I was offered by Anthony Asquith, a dear, dear friend of mine, the film *Orders To Kill*, because I'd had this experience during the war, and it was about an agent who went out to kill a man and found that he couldn't kill him, and this, along with my other experiences, lead [sic] to *Goldfinger*.'[4]

Dehn was being rather modest here – he didn't just have a 'pretty good view' of such matters, but had in fact been one of Britain's best experts in counter-espionage techniques during the Second World War, if not the best. He had been a senior instructor at SOE's training school in Beaulieu, and co-wrote a manual for the organization's agents, bizarrely enough with Kim Philby. Between 1943 and 1944, he was a senior instructor at Camp X, the centre in Canada set up to train SOE and OSS agents to be inserted behind enemy lines to conduct sabotage operations. Dehn also apparently took part in SOE operations himself, in both France and Norway and, according to John le Carré, was even used as an assassin.[5]

It's sometimes claimed that Dehn and Ian Fleming met each other at Camp X, but there doesn't seem to be any concrete evidence for this assertion. Dehn did cross paths with Fleming later, though. In 1959, he was approached to write the screenplay for *Thunderball* – according to Fleming, he turned down the offer because he wasn't interested in 'this bang, bang, kiss kiss stuff'.[6]

Richard Maibaum's draft of *Goldfinger* had opened with James Bond in black tie watching a dancer stamp her heels in a waterfront nightclub, when a warehouse bursts into flames off-screen. Everyone scatters in turmoil, but 007 stays seated calmly, until Sierra, 'a well-dressed and good-looking young Latin' enters the club and approaches Bond. 'Forgive me for being late,' he says. 'There were last-minute complications.'[7]

Dehn evidently decided it would be more exciting if we saw how the operation to blow up the warehouse had been done – and if Bond were the one doing it. His version of the scene first appears in his draft of December 23 1963, albeit in a less playful form than the version filmed: the 'hairless distended cadaver of a dead dog, legs pointing stiffly skyward' drifts through water 'scummed with flotsam, refuse and vegetable rind'. The dead dog then rises clear of the water, revealing James Bond with his teeth 'clamped to the cadaver's underbelly'.[8]

This was deemed too grotesque, and the dead dog became a seagull in the film. But the scene is otherwise almost identical to the finished product. Bond comes ashore in 'a black water proof suit, zip-pocketed all over and a water proof ruck-sack', dispatches a couple of sentries, breaks into a storage tank, squeezes gelignite 'like toothpaste from a stocking', then clears the wall and reaches comparative safety. Then, 'in one smart gesture', he unzips the top of his waterproof suit, revealing a white dinner jacket 'complete with red carnation.'

Paul Dehn knew a lot about the use of gelignite, attacking storage tanks, and inserting secret agents into enemy territory. Camp X's syllabus, which he co-wrote and taught, contained detailed instructions on how to kill sentries silently, place explosives in storage tanks and camouflage oneself when crossing water. Here are three passages on those subjects from the manual:

> 'Killing a sentry, if you are armed with a knife.
> Attack from the rear. With left forearm, strike violently on left side of opponent's neck and instantly transfer the left hand to cover his mouth and nostrils. Simultaneously with the blow on the neck, thrust the knife (held in the right hand) into his kidneys. If equipment interferes with the kidney thrust, bring the hand round to the front and thrust into the abdomen. Note that once the left hand covers mouth and nostrils, the adversary is dragged backwards and downwards...'

> 'Rivers.
> When the stream is deep and slow moving try to find a ford. A good point to cross is at a bend — there is often a gravel bottom and firm ground on both banks. Also it is more difficult for people to see you. Use driftwood or floating vegetation to camouflage the head. If you swim, try to land

amongst rushes or beneath overhanging trees. But ensure that the bank is not too steep to climb...'

'Attacking Storage Tanks.
i) Tanks below ground extremely difficult to tackle.
ii) Above-ground Tanks are often surrounded with anti-blast brick walls and inaccessible except near the inlet valve. In principle the method of attack will always be to get the fuel out into the air, having arranged an incendiary parcel or several individual incendiaries to receive and set fire to the fuel...'[9]

The scene is also reminiscent of the raids conducted by SOE-trained commandos against Vemork power station in Telemark, Norway. In Operation GUNNERSIDE, carried out in February 1943, the commandos infiltrated the power station and placed explosive charges on the heavy water electrolysis chambers. Dehn gave Bond an SOE-style operation, but the manner in which he is inserted was one used by MI6 of which SOE had been envious.

PETER TAZELAAR UNDERTOOK his mission in November 1941 with MI6, but joined SOE later in the war. Following his brief capture by the Germans in January 1942, his use as an agent in Scheveningen was over. After escaping via Switzerland and Spain, he made his way back to Britain in April 1942, whereupon he was promptly dismissed from the Dutch navy for insubordination, a victim of political intrigues beyond his control. After a stint with the Commandos, Tazelaar also became a training instructor in Canada, at the Dutch military base in Guelph, following which he was recruited by SOE and parachuted back into Holland in 1944, from where he maintained radio contact with London for six months.

There is no evidence Dehn ever met Tazelaar, either in England or Canada, but it seems very likely he would have heard about such a remarkable operation from colleagues either during or after the war. One possible occasion came the year before he started work on *Goldfinger*. In December 1962, former SOE officer William Deakin organized a conference on wartime resistance in Europe at St Antony's College, Oxford, of which he was warden. One of the lectures was by Dr Louis de Jong, the director of Holland's State Institute for War Documentation, and in it he described Tazelaar's 'evening dress' operation in detail. De Jong's lecture was published in the proceedings of the conference in a limited mimeograph of fewer than 100 copies.[10] It may be that Dehn attended the conference or read de Jong's lecture in the proceedings afterwards.

At any rate, the idea of the operation seems much too bizarre to have been thought up independently twice, and the fact that Dehn had not only been a senior figure in British intelligence during the Second World War but included several other very specific references to real wartime espionage in the scene points to it being a deliberate reference. It seems likely that, one way or another, Paul Dehn heard of this MI6 operation through his contacts in Britain's close-knit intelligence community, among whom it was a cause célèbre, and decided it was just the sort of daring mission suitable for James Bond. In drawing on real espionage history and expertise, Dehn created a sensational opening sequence that would become an iconic cinematic moment, but perhaps also paid secret tribute to the ingenuity and bravery of Allied secret agents he had worked with and heard about during the war. If so, that would have been very much in the spirit of Ian Fleming, who did much the same in his novels.

In the years immediately following the Second World War, there were dozens of books and films celebrating the derring-do of the Allies, and Fleming's novels were part of that tradition, as were the films adapted from them. Paul Dehn's use of real-life espionage techniques in his screenplay for *Goldfinger* also undermines the widespread perception of the Bond films as unadulterated fantasies, or in the dry words of M in his obituary for 007 in *You Only Live Twice*, 'high-flown and romanticized caricatures' of the intelligence world.

Dehn went on to work on the screenplays for *The Spy Who Came in from the Cold*, *The Deadly Affair* and several other films. He died in 1976. There are still gaps in his secret career we don't know today: curiously, his SOE file still hasn't been declassified.

Erik Hazelhoff Roelfzema continued to run operations on the coast of Holland, inserting agents, weapons and transmitters, before joining the Royal Air Force – he flew 72 missions in a Mosquito and was awarded the Distinguished Flying Cross, as well as the Militaire Willemsorde, the Netherlands' highest military decoration. After the war, he emigrated to the United States. His autobiography, *Soldaat van Oranje* ('Soldier of Orange'), was published in 1971 and was made into a film by Paul Verhoeven in 1977, with Rutger Hauer starring as a fictionalised version of him and Jeroen Krabbé as a composite of several characters, including Peter Tazelaar. Edward Fox played a version of Euan 'The Rabbi' Rabagliati.

Soldier of Orange was the most expensive Dutch film made to date, and helped pave the way for Verhoeven and

Hauer's careers in Hollywood. It was also a calling card for Krabbé, and brought him to the attention of the James Bond films' producers, leading to him playing the role of Koskov in *The Living Daylights*.[11]

In 2003, Hazelhoff Roelfzema published *In Pursuit Of Life*, an expanded autobiography in English, including most of the material from *Soldier of Orange*. The introduction was by Len Deighton. Hazelhoff Roelfzema died in Hawaii in 2007.

Bob van der Stok also joined the RAF, but his Spitfire was shot down in France in 1942 and he was captured by the Germans. He was imprisoned in Stalag Luft III, but was one of the three men to tunnel his way out. In the film *The Great Escape*, James Coburn's character was partly based on van der Stok. He died in 1993.

Peter Tazelaar's life could have provided enough material for several films. Queen Wilhelmina also awarded him the Militaire Willemsorde, and in May 1945 he and Hazelhoff Roelfzema became her aides de camp. Tazelaar wasn't satisfied with that, though, and went off to Ceylon (now Sri Lanka) to fight the Japanese. After that, he served with the military police during the Dutch colonial war in Indonesia, then became a CIA agent, carrying out several missions in eastern and central Europe during the 1950s. He died in 1993.

'He had a lot in common with James Bond,' says Victor Laurentius, author of the biography *De Grote Tazelaar: Ridder & Rebel* ('The Great Tazelaar: Knight and Rebel'). 'He was good looking, a cool womanizer, and in many ways an atypical spy.' Laurentius points out that, like Bond, Tazelaar was an inveterate daredevil: during his operations, he spent significant amounts of time in casinos and other places crowded by German officers.[12]

Real espionage is of course much less glamorous than a Bond film, even if you're wearing black tie. Peter Tazelaar was one of the lucky ones: many Dutch agents ended up captured, tortured and shot. Nevertheless, his remarkable brandy-soaked stroll past the sentries at Scheveningen stands as one of the most imaginative and daring espionage operations of the Second World War. Next time you watch *Goldfinger*, spare a thought for the real spy who dared to journey behind enemy lines in a dinner jacket.

Notes for this chapter:

1. Unless otherwise noted, details about the operation and the careers of those involved are all from *Soldier of Orange* (Sphere, 1982) and *In Pursuit of Life* (Sutton, 2003), both by Erik Hazelhoff Roelfzema, and *De Grote Tazelaar, Ridder & Rebel* by Victor Laurentius (Stichting Peter Tazelaar, 2010).
2. Hamilton to author, March 11 2010.
3. *SOE: The Special Operations Executive, 1940-1946* by M.R.D. Foot, (BBC, 1984), p86.
4. *Cinefantasique Planet of the Apes* special issue, summer 1972.
5. *How to be a Spy: The World War II SOE Training Manual* (PRO, 2004) introduced by Denis Rigden, p17; *Beaulieu: Finishing School for Secret Agents* by Cyril Cunningham (Pen & Sword, 2005) pix; interview with John le Carré on *The Spy Who Came In From The Cold* Criterion Collection DVD, 2008.
6. *The Battle for Bond* by Robert Sellers (Tomahawk Press, 2008), p29.
7. Maibaum draft of *Goldfinger*, Special Collections, University of Iowa Libraries.
8. This and subsequent quotes from Dehn's draft of *Goldfinger*, December 23 1963, Special Collections, University of Iowa Libraries.

9. All from *How to be a Spy: The World War II SOE Training Manual* (PRO, 2004) introduced by Denis Rigden.
10. *Britain and Dutch Resistance, 1940-1945* by Louis de Jong (delivered at a conference on Britain and European resistance, St Anthony's College, Oxford, December 10-16, 1962).
11. Michael G. Wilson in the documentary *Inside The Living Daylights*, John Cork and Bruce Scivally, 2000.
12. Laurentius to author, February 11 2010.

SMERSH vs SMERSH

'SMERSH.'

The word just *sounds* sinister. It instantly conjures up an image of the Soviet Union, the Cold War and, of course, James Bond.

Many presume that the organisation was invented by Ian Fleming, but SMERSH really existed – albeit in a somewhat different form than that described in his novels. Fleming never revealed precisely where he learned about SMERSH, although according to John Pearson's biography, he first came across it in 'a magazine article soon after the war, and he embroidered on what little information he had about the organization and introduced it melodramatically into *Casino Royale*.'[1]

If so, this would probably have been in connection with *SMERSH* by Nicola Sinevirsky, which was published in English in 1950. It was at around this time that Fleming was trying to introduce himself into literary circles more prominently, meeting Jonathan Cape, Edith Sitwell and William Plomer, and keeping up with all the latest literary magazines.[2] So one candidate for the book coming to his attention is *The Saturday Review of Literature*, which ran a review of it by its Eastern European expert Hal Lehrman in its issue of November 25 1950. The same issue had Winston Churchill on the cover in connection with the latest installment of his autobiography, and included reviews of Vladimir 'Popski' Peniakoff's memoirs and Ludwig Moyzisch's *Operation Cicero*. Fleming was fascinated by all three of those subjects. Churchill's obituary of his father was on display wherever he lived in his later years; he had met Popski at the Savoy Hotel in London to discuss his book at the request of Jonathan Cape; and Operation Cicero was mentioned in *Moonraker*, while the attempted assassination of Van Papen in Ankara a year before the affair would inspire the 'men in straw hats' incident in *Casino Royale*.

SMERSH was the first book to name the organisation. Sinevirsky was a pseudonym for Mikhail Mondich, a Ruthenian member of an anti-communist group called the National Alliance of Russian Solidarists, or NTS. He claimed to have infiltrated SMERSH and worked undercover in the organization for seven months before escaping to West Germany where, in 1948, the NTS newspaper *Possev* published his diary. The 1950 English translation of *SMERSH* published by Henry Holt & Company was an edited version of Mondich's diary that had been put together by two American journalist brothers, Kermit and Milt Hill. Lehrman's review of the book was dismissive:

> 'Dragooned into the Soviet Army, [Mondich] is accidentally drafted as interpreter for – guess what – the secret police. Sinevirsky, his editors, and publishers think it is something new and special called SMERSH... but it is really just an NKVD counter-espionage branch.'[3]

Despite this, it appears Fleming was intrigued enough to seek out the book himself, because when he started writing *Casino Royale* 14 months later,[4] he drew much of his material for SMERSH directly from it. Mondich's book had been published in the United States at the height of McCarthyism and fears of Communism. As a result, the emphasis was very much on the propaganda benefits of a first-hand account of Soviet brutality. The back cover hailed the book as being 'of vital significance to an America that is already engaged in a political struggle against Bolshevik aggression', while the flyleaf proclaimed:

> 'This book reveals for the first time the intimate details of Stalin's secret weapon – Smersh. What is it? What does it mean? It means "Death to Spies" and is a contraction of the Russian words, Smert Shpionam… It is the new supersecret counter-espionage elite whose creed is "Let thousands of innocents die lest one guilty go free!" Its weapons are terror and fear and unbelievable brutality. It is the absolute of depravity, degeneration, and the power-corruption which is Russia today…'

It's not hard to see why this would have appealed to Ian Fleming – for an aspiring thriller-writer, a 'new supersecret counter-espionage elite' must have been like manna from heaven. As an experienced journalist, Fleming was constantly scouring the world around him for tidbits of information he could process and transform into gold. In his 1963 article 'How to Write a Thriller', he revealed a little of his methodology:

> 'You must know thrilling things before you can write about them. Imagination alone isn't enough, but stories you hear from friends or read in the papers can be built up by a fertile imagination and

a certain amount of research and documentation into incidents that will also ring true in fiction.'[5]

Pearson noted that experts on Soviet affairs were quick to point out that 'SMERSH was really a body which worked very largely with the Red Army during the war, rounding up German spies and saboteurs and Russian traitors, that it was a mistake to think that it had operated outside the borders of the U.S.S.R., that it was never a counter-intelligence unit in the sense that it worked against enemy secret services, and that in any case it had changed its name at the end of the war. Fleming, who always knew a good thing when he met one, took no notice and continued to base himself on his outdated conception of SMERSH.'

When Fleming started writing *Casino Royale* in early 1952, Mondich's book was the only account of SMERSH's activities to have been published anywhere in the world. However, he might also have had his own sources for information on the organisation: as the assistant to the Director of Naval Intelligence during the Second World War, he was well-placed to hear of counter-intelligence activities. Fleming also established 30 Assault Unit, an intelligence-gathering commando group that followed the Allied troops into Germany, Austria and elsewhere searching for documents and equipment left behind by the Nazis late in the war.[6] SMERSH were active in the same area at the same time, hunting down suspected traitors to the Soviet Union – members of the National Alliance of Russian Solidarists, for instance, as well as Latvian and Ukrainian nationalists who had joined the Waffen SS and the Nazis' mobile killing squads.[7]

But even with Fleming's war work, it seems highly unlikely that he would have had the level of detailed knowledge about SMERSH's structure that is depicted in Mondich's book – especially as a study of it reveals that Fleming seems to have drawn his material in *Casino Royale* directly from it. Mondich omitted the fact that SMERSH was no longer operating under that name by 1950 – it was disbanded and all its duties handed over to the Main Administration of Counter-Intelligence (GUKR) of the MGB in 1946[8] – presumably because any mention of this would have greatly lessened his book's impact. *Casino Royale* also features a still-active SMERSH, albeit with the proviso that it has been reduced in size. Mondich provided the basic background material on the organization, but Fleming made sure he adapted it to make it more thrilling.

In Chapter 6 of his book, Mondich gave a complete rundown of the organization's structure:

> 'SMERSH counter-intelligence, I learned, was divided into five departments.'[9]

When it came to writing MI6's dossier on SMERSH in *Casino Royale*, Fleming followed these pages very closely:

> 'The organization itself was thoroughly purged after the war and is now believed to consist of only a few hundred operatives of very high quality divided into five sections.'

According to Mondich, the First Department was attached directly to the front, where it monitored political trends inside the Red Army. Fleming rendered this as:

'Department I: In charge of counter intelligence among Soviet organizations at home and abroad.'

This is both broader and vaguer in scope. Perhaps the idea of a super-secret elite working in ordinary uniforms as informers at the front didn't seem as thrilling.

Fleming adapted the other departments' roles into similarly concise and exciting prose. The Second Department, according to Mondich, was Operations, which was responsible for seeking out 'organised enemies of the system'. Anyone suspected of committing a crime against the Soviet Union 'must die'. Fleming neatly summarised this as:

'Department II: Operations, including executions.'[10]

Mondich claimed that the Third Department was Administrative, but that he knew little about it, that the Fourth was the Investigation Department, and that the Fifth was the Prosecuting Department. Confusingly, he then mentioned two further departments, the Personnel Department and the Finance Department, which makes seven, not five. Fleming got round this by adding Finance to Department Three and Personnel to Department Four:

'Department III: Administration and Finance.
Department IV: Investigations and legal work. Personnel.
Department V: Prosecutions: the section which passes final judgement on all victims.'

Mondich also claimed that SMERSH's headquarters were in Moscow. Perhaps this seemed too predictable, because Fleming placed them in Leningrad instead, with a sub-station in Moscow (although he would change this in *From Russia, With Love*). He also attributed Trotsky's assassination to the organisation, even though it took place a year before it was formed (a mistake many subsequent writers have repeated). And instead of being 'Stalin's secret weapon', Fleming wrote that it was 'believed to come under the personal direction of Beria'.[11]

One thing Fleming did not alter from Mondich's book was its trumpeted information about the meaning of the organization's name:

> 'SMERSH is a conjunction of two Russian words: 'Smyert Shpionam', meaning roughly: "Death to Spies".'

As John Pearson noted, Ian Fleming knew a good thing when he met one.

FLEMING'S USE OF SMERSH in *Casino Royale* was a masterstroke: right at the start of the Cold War, he stole a march on the legions of thriller-writers who would follow him, almost all of whom would use branches of the MVD or the KGB as the enemy. By settling on a little-known Soviet intelligence group instead, Fleming invested his work with an aura of originality and inside knowledge that would 'ring true in fiction'. At the same time, he put his own stamp on the genre – nobody else could use SMERSH after him without seeming unoriginal.

Fleming also cleverly – and unusually for a thriller-writer of his era – ignored the crude propagandistic elements of his source material. In Chapter Nine of *Casino Royale*, we learn that in order to join the prestigious Double O Section of the British Secret Service James Bond assassinated two men, one of whom was a double agent. The elimination of treachery, then, is something that MI6's Double O Section has in common with SMERSH's Department II, which seeks out 'organised enemies of the system' and kills them.[12]

But Fleming didn't stop there: although Bond casually tells Vesper Lynd over caviar and hot toast that he has killed in cold blood, after he is tortured by the villain, Le Chiffre, he reappraises the situation, admitting to Mathis that the Norwegian traitor he killed 'just didn't die very quickly', and agonising over 'the nature of evil', as the chapter title puts it:

> 'Take our friend Le Chiffre. It's easy enough to say he's an evil man, at least it's simple enough for me because he did evil things to me. If he was here now, I wouldn't hesitate to kill him, but out of personal revenge and not, I'm afraid, for some high moral reason or for the sake of my country.'

Bond's anxieties here — and the confusion of hero and villain and patriotism and personal motive — may have been influenced by Geoffrey Household's classic 1939 thriller *Rogue Male*, in which the narrator, trapped in an underground burrow, is forced to face the fact that he is not morally superior to his tormentor, a tall, fair-haired Nazi officer who has taken on the cover role of an English gentleman, 'Major Quive-Smith', and repeatedly calls him 'my dear fellow'. In the first chapter of *Rogue Male*, the narrator tries to assassinate Hitler, but the shot misses due to a sudden change in the wind: later, as he is questioned by 'Quive-Smith' on his motivation for the assassination attempt, we learn that it was not out of a sense of patriotism or some high moral reason, but the fact that the Germans had shot his lover:

> 'I declared war upon the men who could commit such sacrilege, and above all upon the man who has given them their creed. How ridiculous that one person should declare war upon a nation! That was another reason I hid from myself what I was doing. My war was a futile cause to me, to be smiled at sympathetically just as I used to smile at her enthusiasms. Yet in fact my war is anything but futile. Its cost

in lives and human suffering is low. Seek out and destroy the main body of the enemy – and I should have destroyed it but for a change of wind.'[13]

This theme is echoed in the final chapter of *Casino Royale*, in which James Bond vows to go after the men who engineered the death of his lover, Vesper Lynd:

> 'SMERSH was the spur. Be faithful, spy well, or you die. Inevitably and without question, you will be hunted down and killed.
> It was the same with the whole Russian machine. Fear was the impulse. For them it was always safer to advance than retreat. Advance against the enemy and the bullet might miss you. Retreat, evade, betray, and the bullet would never miss. But now he would attack the arm that held the whip and the gun. The business of espionage could be left to the white-collar boys. They could spy, and catch the spies. He would go after the threat behind the spies, the threat that made them spy.'

Such nuanced delineations are rare in espionage thrillers written so soon after the Second World War, and the popular perception of Fleming as a gung-ho patriot often fails to address these moments in *Casino Royale*. This is partly of Fleming's own doing, though, because in his second novel, *Live And Let Die*, he discarded the hard-earned lessons Bond had learned in the first book. And just as the scar on Bond's hand is erased, so too is the research of the first novel: SMERSH did not employ foreign gangsters. In *Live And Let Die*, Fleming moved his depiction of the organization from broadly reflecting the role it played in reality – the hunter of enemies of the Soviet state – to a more amorphous, if still gloriously sinister-sounding, 'red menace'.

SMERSH is only tangential to the plot of *Live And Let Die*, but for its next appearance in a Bond novel it took centre-stage. In *From Russia, With Love*, Fleming brought all his skills to bear to create perhaps the most famous depiction of a villainous organisation in fiction.[14] Fleming now used the Russian word 'Otdely' instead of Department, and heading up Otdely II – memorably described by Tatania Romanova as 'the very whisper of death' – he introduced the fearsome Rosa Klebb.

Fleming's interest in SMERSH had been reignited by the case of the Russian cipher expert Vladimir Petrov, who had defected to Australia in 1954. Writing about the case in his *Sunday Times* column 'Atticus', Fleming brought in his knowledge of Beria's 'messengers of death' and also mentioned a mysterious 'Madame Rybkin', who he thought might be the most powerful woman in espionage.

Colonel Zoya Rybkina, alias 'Madam Yartseva', was the head of the NKVD's German section throughout World War Two.[15] She discovered the Nazis' plan to attack the Soviet Union in June 1941 and told Stalin about it five days before the invasion – he didn't believe her.[16] Under the name Zoya Voskresenskaya, Rybkina later became famous in Russia as a children's writer with a series of stories following the adventures of Lenin as a boy, two of which were made into successful films. Fleming may also have been inspired by a description Rachel Terry had given him of Emma Wolff, a hideous NKVD agent based in Vienna, adding some of her physical attributes to Klebb.[17]

One final inspiration for Klebb may have been Major Tamara Nicolayeva Ivanova, one of Russian intelligence's 'few female high officials' and 'an over-worked nervous spinster', according to *Soviet Spy Net* by E.H. Cookridge.[18]

Cookridge was a pseudonym for former British agent Edward Spiro, and this book, published in Britain in 1955, was a highly coloured account of the activities of Russian intelligence agencies around the world – according to Henry Chancellor, Fleming used it as the background source for most of his Cold War novels.[19]

Although it only mentions SMERSH once, and that's on the first page of its introduction to state that it no longer exists, this book contains the germs of many of Fleming's greatest ideas. Ivanova is also only mentioned once, but Spiro claimed she was an instructor of Captain Nicolai Evgenyevich Khokhlov, the MVD agent who defected to the Americans in Germany in 1954, claiming to have been sent to assassinate Georgi Okolovich, chairman of the NTS in Frankfurt. Khokhlov is mentioned several times in *From Russia, With Love*, and is central to Fleming's construction of the book. In Chapter Three, the entirely fictional General Grubozaboyschikov tells the real Serov "We don't want another Khokhlov affair", while in Chapter 26, Bond is told that his current predicament will 'knock spots' off the Khokhlov case.[20]

Spiro claimed that Khokhlov was a member of the MVD's 'Otydel for Terror and Diversion', and gave a graphic account of this division's activities, most of which has never appeared in any creditable non-fiction work about Soviet intelligence. Chapter Eight of the book is dedicated to training, and reveals the general syllabus taught to MVD agents between 1948 and 1953, including the principles of Marxism, the history of other systems of government, 'the Problems of Negroes and other Colonial Peoples', codes and ciphers, and physical training:

'Lt. Colonel Nicolai Godlovsky, director of the Cheka small arms section, is the Soviet rifle marksmanship champion... The training for the budding "executioners" is carried out in a barrack-like building on the corner of Metrostroveskaya Sreet and Turnaninsky Pereulok in Moscow. The director of this training establishment is Colonel of the M.V.D., Arkady Foyotev. The syllabus includes rifle and pistol shooting, driving (motor-cars and motor-cycles), judo, boxing, photography and elementary courses in radio technique. This course is only for beginners. Graduates of the "Section for Terror and Diversion" are trained at special establishment at Kuchino, a large country house outside Moscow, where they are prepared for their "special tasks", and for which the syllabus includes the use of special weapons and poisons.'[21]

Fleming used this chapter as the basis for Donovan 'Red' Grant's training, attributing the MVD's methods to his imaginary version of a still-active SMERSH:

'The next year was spent, with only two other foreign students among several hundred Russians, at the School for Terror and Diversion at Kuchino, outside Moscow. Here Grant went triumphantly through courses in judo, boxing, athletics, photography and radio under the general supervision of the famous Colonel Arkady Fotoyev, father of the modern Soviet spy, and completed his small-arms instruction at the hands of Lieutenant-Colonel Nikolai Godlovsky, the Soviet Rifle Champion.'

Quite apart from switching all this to SMERSH, Fleming adapted Spiro's text in such a way that even if it had been true, it could no longer be. Spiro listed judo, boxing and so on as being taught to beginners, with only graduates moving on to Kuchino. Perhaps because the details of the beginners' course were more compelling and more concrete than the much vaguer description of the graduate course, Fleming listed the beginners' activities as being taught at the graduates' school. In doing so, he got all the authentic-sounding material in – all the activities taught, the names of both instructors, the menacing name of the school and the place-name – even though it meant contradicting his source.

Fleming's aim was not to describe the inner workings of Soviet espionage accurately, but convincingly. He was writing novels, not non-fiction, and he used artistic licence as and when he saw fit. The details he used sound authoritative, and lure us into believing we are in the hands of a true espionage insider.

Fleming also built cleverly on the true circumstances. Khokhlov was a genuine agent, but he had defected before completing his assassination mission. In Red Grant, Fleming created a rather less squeamish opponent for Bond:

> 'SMERSH has made one or two mistakes lately. That Khokhlov business for one. Remember the explosive cigarette case and all that? Gave it to the wrong man. Should have given it to me. I wouldn't have gone over to the Yanks.'[2]

Khokhlov did not work for SMERSH, of course, but when he defected he brought with him an array of weapons, including a cigarette case that fired dum-dum bullets through the tips and an electrically fired miniature revolver that could be hidden in the palm of a hand: it was a propaganda coup the Americans fully exploited, showing off both the would-be assassin and his paraphernalia at a packed press conference at the American High Commission in Bonn on April 22, 1954.

Spiro commented on the case as follows:

> 'It was said that if a popular writer of thrillers had invented a tale of disguised secret agents carrying such weapons to kill their victim in the centre of a European city, even ardent readers would say the story was incredible. But, in fact, these

things have been done, and done successfully, by Cheka agents before.'[22]

Such a sentiment must have been almost a provocation to Ian Fleming! Not only did he give Red Grant an even more fanciful weapon, hidden inside a copy of War and Peace, he took Spiro's line and ran with it. In *How to Write a Thriller*, he wrote that his plots were 'fantastic, while being based upon truth':

> 'They go wildly beyond the probable but not beyond the possible. Every now and then there will be a story in the newspapers that lifts a corner of the veil from Secret Service work. A tunnel from West to East Berlin so that our Secret Service can tap the Russian telephone system: the Russian spy Khokhlov with his cigarette case that fired dum-dum bullets; "The Man Who Never Was" – the corpse with the false invasion plans that we left for the Gestapo to find. This is all true Secret Service history that is yet in the higher realm of fantasy, and James Bond's ventures into this realm are perfectly legitimate.'

The idea of using a tunnel to listen in on the Russians also made its way into *From Russia, With Love*, incidentally, albeit on a much smaller scale than the technical feat that was Operation GOLD: Darko Kerim and James Bond eavesdrop on a Soviet meeting with a submarine periscope while standing in Istanbul's sewers. Kerim mentions that Q Branch are trying to find a way to wire the periscope for sound.

Fleming's insistence that his work was 'based upon truth' and 'not beyond the possible' is nevertheless intriguing. Firstly, Spiro's book was not the truth, and Fleming, an experienced journalist, must have suspected that. Even if he took it all to be true, Spiro only mentioned SMERSH once in his book, where he said it no longer exists. Fleming either didn't read Spiro's introduction or disregarded it, feeling that the defunct SMERSH sounded more exciting than the real MVD — and as he had already used it in *Casino Royale*, it was his organization, in a way.

A more ingenious example of the way Fleming used research is evident from Grant's cover identity, Captain Norman Nash. Grant posing as an English gentleman and repeatedly calling Bond 'old man' appears to be a further reference to *Rogue Male* and 'Major Quive-Smith'. And, as Henry Chancellor has pointed out, Fleming took his surname from the glossary of terms in Spiro's book:

> '"Nash": "Ours", Cheka description for a sympathiser or potential informant.'[23]

Fleming has Tania tell Bond this, presaging the revelation that 'Nash' is not all he seems:

> '"What did you say his name is?"
> "Nash. Norman Nash."
> She spelled it out. "N.A.S.H.? Like that?"
> "Yes."
> The girl's eyes were puzzled. "I suppose you know what that means in Russian. Nash means 'ours'. In our Services, a man is *nash* when he is one of 'our' men. He is *svoi* when he is one of 'theirs' — when he belongs to the enemy. And this man calls himself Nash. That is not pleasant."'

Tatiana Romanova doesn't appear to have any direct historical counterpart, but much of her background is also taken from Spiro's book; it contains a chapter on the Central Index, where Tania works, which we are told mostly employs women. This is also where Fleming found the information about the Russians' files, *zapiski*, the Russian for 'top secret', and many other details. But while most thriller-writers research to make their fiction as realistic as possible, Fleming was concerned if it was interesting first, and plausible second. He also used his research material as a jumping-off point for ideas. As well as providing Fleming with a lot of authoritative-sounding jargon, Spiro's book seems to have triggered plot ideas. In a passage about the use of mercenary spies, Spiro wrote:

> 'The conflict of the hot and cold war ideologies since 1939 has resulted in the eclipse of the professional "free lance" spy, beloved of the pre-war thriller writers – the Mata Haris and the glamorous blondes of the Orient Express.'[24]

There were indeed many thrillers predating the 1950s that featured beautiful female agents and the most famous train in the world – but perhaps this was the trigger for Fleming to write his own variation of the form.

A few lines later, Spiro discussed the exploits of the Switz Gang, a syndicate of spies who trapped leading French officials into revealing defence secrets, which they then sold to both the Nazis and the Soviets:

> 'It was as romantic as any thriller lover could desire. A few blonde hairs adhering to a roll of camera film, which fell into the hands of the Deuxième Bureau, was the clue that led counter-espionage agents, with the help of Scotland Yard, to Mrs. Marjorie Switz.'[25]

As well as the echoes of the photo blackmail plot in *From Russia, With Love*, the Switz Gang sounds like it might also have been an inspiration for S.P.E.C.T.R.E. in *Thunderball*.

FLEMING CHEEKILY PREFACED *From Russia, With Love* with a note insisting on the accuracy of the information about SMERSH contained within the novel. Apart from sheer bravado – the organization had been disbanded over a decade earlier – this may have been because he was helped with his research by the Russian rocket scientist Grigori Tokaev, who had defected to Britain in 1947.[26] Tokaev — who later took the name Tokaty — was the only Soviet official to defect to Britain between 1945 and 1963. But while he had some knowledge of Russia's intelligence structure, he had never been a member of SMERSH; he also spent much of his time in Britain assisting the Information Research Department, a secret group within the Foreign Office that created anti-Communist propaganda.[27]

Fleming was happy to chop and change information as it suited him. The truth was a starting point, and it was always more important that it sounded like it could be true than whether it was. And a little note at the start would be enough to convince most people that it was the truth, and that they had been given an insider's glimpse into the espionage world. As we can see, that was hardly the case. Far from being an accurate description of the workings of SMERSH, the 'most secret department of the Soviet government', as Fleming claimed in his author's note, *From Russia, With Love* in fact gives an exciting but rather inaccurate representation of the workings of another Soviet organization entirely, the MVD, based on a publicly available account that itself was dubious, even before he attributed its methods to the long-defunct SMERSH.

Regardless of historical accuracy, *From Russia, With Love* established SMERSH as spy fiction's greatest villains to date. Considering the wealth of projects that exploited the success of Bond in the '60s, it seems surprising that there weren't more books about SMERSH during this period. One reason, of course, was the difficulty in getting hold of first-hand information.

One book claiming to offer this is *Nights Are Longest There: SMERSH From The Inside* by A.I. Romanov, which was published in English in 1972. 'Romanov' – a fitting pseudonym – writes that he was recruited into Department I during the war, meaning that we get lots of insight into life on the front-lines, as well as a thorough history of the organisation. It's a world away from Fleming: Romanov spent most of his time questioning people about garrisons and troop movements in hutments, occasionally being dragged out to a forest with his comrades to witness an execution. And where Mikhail Mondich verged on the hysterical, Romanov takes understatement to excess:

> 'In Poland... I witnessed the execution of one of our officers, who had raped a young Polish girl in her parents' home. The order of sentence in this case was widely publicised, both to our forces and the local population. Later, in Budapest, I was present when a group of leaders of the Hungarian pro-fascist party 'Crossed Arrows' was hanged. All these scenes left me with an impression that can in no way be described as pleasant.'[28]

IAN FLEMING ONLY used SMERSH once again: Auric Goldfinger is its treasurer. But here, as in *Live And Let Die*, this was more a convenient prop to explain Bond's interest in the mission than anything else. And in his next novel, *Thunderball*, Fleming finally did away with SMERSH altogether, replacing it with the wholly fictional S.P.E.C.T.R.E. In an interview given to *Playboy* shortly before his death, Fleming gave his reasons:

> 'I closed down SMERSH, although I was devoted to the good old apparat, because, first of all, Khrushchev did in fact disband SMERSH himself, although its operations are still

carried out by a subsection of the K.G.B., the Russian secret service. But in that book – I think it was *Thunderball* that I was writing at the time of the proposed summit meeting – I thought well, it's no good going on if we're going to make friends with the Russians. I know them, I like them personally, as anyone would, as anyone would like the Chinese if he knew them. I thought, I don't want to go on ragging them like this. So I invented S.P.E.C.T.R.E. as an international crime organisation which contained elements of SMERSH and the Gestapo and the Mafia – the cosy old Cosa Nostra – which, of course, is a much more elastic fictional device than SMERSH, which was no fictional device, but the real thing.'[29]

The makers of the Bond films felt the same, preferring to use the elastic S.P.E.C.T.R.E. than the real-life SMERSH (and *SPECTRE* is the title of the next film, due out in 2015). But the idea that a 'subsection of the KGB' might still be carrying out SMERSH's duties (which, in fact, it had been before Fleming started writing about it) found favour with John Gardner when he came to write his James Bond novels. In *Icebreaker*, SMERSH was transformed into 'Department V'. This was a real subsection of the KGB, although it was in fact descended from the Special Administration of Special Tasks, a sabotage and assassination division during the Second World War often confused with SMERSH, rather than from SMERSH itself. However, as with Fleming, historical accuracy was not the name of the game, and Gardner took his readers back to Fleming's original fascination with this strange, sinister Soviet group:

"'Smersh has what I understand is called, in criminal parlance, a hit list. That list includes a number of names – people who are wanted, not dead but alive. Can you imagine whose name is number one on the chart, James Bond?"'[30]

If such hit lists seem 'beyond the possible', one only has to consider the fate of Nicolai Khokhlov, whose case so inspired Fleming when writing *From Russia, With Love*. That novel ends with James Bond being poisoned by a kick from Rosa Klebb. Five months after it was published, in September 1957, Khokhlov himself was poisoned with the metal thallium, which had been inserted into a cup of coffee. He eventually recovered, but not before he had gone bald, blood had seeped through his pores and his entire body had become disfigured with black-and-blue swellings. The obvious similarities to the cases of both Viktor Yushchenko and Alexander Litvinenko suggest that Ian Fleming's conception of the Russian secret services may not have been so wide of the mark after all.

Notes for this chapter:

1. *The Life of Ian Fleming* by John Pearson (The Companion Book Club, 1966), p285.
2. Pearson, p184.
3. eg 'NKVD Counter-Espionage', *Saturday Review of Literature*, November 25 1950, p40.
4. Pearson, p203.
5. 'How to Write a Thriller' by Ian Fleming, *Books and Bookmen*, May 1963.
6. *Ian Fleming* by Andrew Lycett (Phoenix, 2002), p156.
7. SMERSH screened over five million people during this time, including Soviet POWs – many were transported to the gulags and died. The British government aided the 'freeing' of Soviet POWs, later claiming not to be aware of the fate awaiting them, most controversially forcibly repatriating the Cossacks held at Lienz in Austria, an incident that forms part of the plot of the film Goldeneye. In June 1945, SMERSH managed to track down a group of Cossack White generals in the area; KGB defector Vasili Mitrokhin claimed in 1999 that the SMERSH men were aided by the British, bribing a

lieutenant-colonel with fourteen kilograms of gold to arrange their capture. SMERSH photographers recorded the handover. One wonders if Fleming had heard about this incident, as some of the elements of it are similar to events in his short story *Octopussy*. See *The Sword And The Shield: The Mitrokhin Archive and The Secret History of the KGB*, Christopher Andrew and Vasili Mitrokhin (Basic, 1999), p134-135.

8. *KGB: The Inside Story Of Its Foreign Operations From Lenin To Gorbachev* by Christopher Andrew and Oleg Gordievsky (Sceptre, 1991), pp350-1; and *Nights Are Longest There: SMERSH From The Inside* by A.I. Romanov (Hutchinson, 1972), pp192.

9. *SMERSH* by Nicola Sinevirsky (Henry Holt & Co, 1950), p74.

10. Chapter Two, 'Dossier for M'.

11. Fleming had to refer back to this in *Live and Let Die* because – in events that would seem almost too fantastic for a James Bond novel – Beria was arrested at the push of a secret button at a meeting of the Praesidium in June 1953, and executed, possibly on suspicion of being a British agent, shortly after.

12. 'SMERSH: Soviet Military Counter-Intelligence during the Second World War' by Robert Stephan, *Journal of Contemporary History*, Vol. 22, No. 4, *Intelligence Services during the Second World War: Part 2* (October 1987), pp 585-613.

13. *Rogue Male* by Geoffrey Household (Penguin, 1985), p154.

14. It is perhaps just pipped to the post by S.P.E.C.T.R.E., although the film due in 2015 might make this point moot.

15. 'Court Life Street Life' by Igor Zakharov, *The Moscow Times*, February 15 1997.

16. 'Women Add Glamour to Cloak and Dagger Profession' by Irina Titova, *The St Petersburg Times*, June 25 2004.

17. Lycett, pp290-291.

18. *Soviet Spy Net* by E.H. Cookridge (Frederick Muller, 1955), p161.

19. *James Bond: The Man and His World* by Henry Chancellor (John Murray, 2005), p212.

20. *From Russia With Love* by Ian Fleming (Pan, 1959), p191.

21. Cookridge, p99.

22. Cookridge, pxiii.

23. Cookridge, p91-92.
24. Ibid.
25. Cookridge, p157.
26. Lycett, p84.
27. Obituary of Tokaty in *The Independent*, November 25 2003.
28. Romanov, p98. The book was translated into English by Gerald Brooke, the British lecturer who three years previously had been in the world's spotlight when he was exchanged for the Krogers.
29. 'The Playboy Interview: Ian Fleming' by Ken Purdy, *Playboy*, December 1964.
30. *Icebreaker* by John Gardner (Berkley, 1983), p190.

Bourne Yesterday

'HE HAS A stolid face and solid musculature, which we know because he goes topless more than his leading ladies do. He has vigorous skirmishes on roofs, in cars and in hotel rooms. He takes as severe a beating – and shows as much emotion – as a crash-test dummy. He's a government spy whom his government wants dead, and he's mourning the violent death of his girlfriend. He so resembles another famous agent that you half-expect him to say, "The name is Bourne. Jason Bourne."'[1]

So ran *TIME's* review of the 2008 James Bond film *Quantum of Solace*. It was one of several that felt that the film was imitative of or influenced by the Jason Bourne films starring Matt Damon. The films are loosely based on the novels of the same name by Robert Ludlum, primarily *The Bourne Identity*. Published in 1980, that novel features a man who is shot and falls into the sea, but manages to survive and make it to dry land. His former colleagues presume him dead, but he recovers, with one crucial setback: he has lost his memory, and has no idea that he is in fact a ruthless secret agent. On discovering his identity in a Swiss bank, he is stunned: 'My name's Bourne. Jason Bourne...'[2]

The book was a worldwide best-seller on publication in 1980, as were its two sequels, and a new writer, Eric Van Lustbader, has written several further novels featuring the character since Ludlum's death in 2001. The films took the central premise of Ludlum's novel and fashioned new plots around it, reinvigorating the spy genre in the process. But that premise, of a secret agent on a mission presumed dead at sea, surviving, but discovering he has amnesia, has a surprising legacy of its own – and its most immediate precursor is Ian Fleming.

IN THE CLOSING scenes of Fleming's 1964 novel *You Only Live Twice*, James Bond is on a mission in Japan under cover as a local fisherman when he is hit on the head and plunges into the sea. He survives, but loses his memory:

> 'The tremendous impact with the water had at first knocked all the wind out of Bond, but the will to live, so nearly extinguished by the searing pain in his head, was revived by the new but recognizable enemy of the sea and, when Kissy got to him, he was struggling to free himself from the kimono.
> At first he thought she was Blofeld and tried to strike out at her.
> "It's Kissy," she said urgently, "Kissy Suzuki! Don't you remember?"
> He didn't. He had no recollection of anything in the world but the face of his enemy and of the desperate urge to smash it. But his strength was going and finally, cursing feebly, he allowed her to manhandle him out of the kimono and paid heed to the voice that pleaded with him.
> "Now follow me, Taro-san. When you get tired I will pull you with me. We are all trained in such rescue work."

But, when she started off, Bond didn't follow her. Instead he swam feebly round and round like a wounded animal, in ever-increasing circles. She almost wept. What had happened to him? What had they done to him at the Castle of Death? Finally she stopped him and talked softly to him and he docilely allowed her to put her arms under his armpits and, with his head cradled between her breasts, she set off with the traditional backward leg-stroke.

It was an amazing swim for a girl – half a mile with currents to contend with and only the moon and an occasional glance over her shoulder to give her a bearing, but she achieved it and finally hauled Bond out of the water in her little cove and collapsed on the flat stones beside him.

She was awoken by a groan from Bond. He had been quietly sick and now sat with his head in his hands, looking blankly out to sea with the glazed eyes of a sleepwalker. When Kissy put an arm round his shoulders, he turned vaguely towards her. "Who are you? How did I get here? What is this place?" He examined her more carefully. "You're very pretty."[3]

Bond comes to believe that he is his cover identity, Taro Todoroki. But his amnesia has a very unusual side-effect: he has become a complete innocent in matters of the flesh, having apparently forgotten 'how to perform the act of love'. This is soon remedied, and Bond finally regains a glimmer of memory triggered by seeing the word 'Vladivostok'. The novel ends with him leaving setting off for the Soviet Union, unaware that he is heading straight into enemy territory.

Robert Ludlum was a fan of Ian Fleming. In 1992, he wrote the following in an article for *Entertainment Weekly* on the 30th anniversary of the Bond films:

'Fleming was a contemporary nexus, a vital connection, as well as a necessary contribution, that forced my generation of suspense writers to look deeper into the intrigues — political, geopolitical, and international — than we might have before he arrived in print. Fleming was a bridge over critical waters: He romanticized terrible inequities by obliterating them. But by doing so, he led those who followed him, followed in the wake of the extraordinary promotion and acceptance worldwide of the novels and the movies and eventually the videocassettes, to make those genuine inequities and intrigues perhaps — only perhaps — a touch more literary (a pretentious term, and certainly arguable).'[4]

Ludlum certainly followed Fleming in *The Bourne Identity*. The opening and premise of the novel were both clearly inspired by the ending of *You Only Live Twice*: another writer's musing on the idea of what might happen if James Bond forgot who he was. Fleming himself didn't follow it up particularly satisfactorily; his next and last novel, *The Man With The Golden Gun*, opens with Bond returning to London. As he recaps to M what has happened to him since we last saw him, his journey between Japan and the Soviet Union is not explored:

> "'I'm afraid there's a lot I still can't remember, sir. I got a bang on the head" – he touched his right temple – "somewhere along the line on that job you sent me to do in Japan. Then there's a blank until I got picked up by the police on the waterfront at Vladivostok. No idea how I got there. They roughed me up a bit and in the process I must have got another bang on the head because suddenly I remembered who I was and that I wasn't a Japanese fisherman which was what I thought I was.'"[5]

Bond has in fact been brainwashed by the Soviets and sent to London to kill M. When this fails, he is swiftly unbrainwashed and sent on a new mission, and his amnesia is never mentioned again. It seems Robert Ludlum felt that there was more mileage to be had from the premise, and spun out a new story along the lines of what a James Bond who had lost his memory might have gone through between leaving Japan and ending up on the waterfront at Vladivostok. Ludlum made his character an American agent and gave him some different characteristics from Bond, but the core idea is the same, and both Jason Bourne's initials and the wording of his discovery of his identity make the homage to Fleming clear.

BUT, IRONICALLY, IT seems that Ian Fleming's idea for James Bond to lose his memory may *also* have had its roots in previous thrillers. In Dennis Wheatley's novel *Faked Passports*, published in June 1940, British secret agent Gregory Sallust travels to Petsamo where, after taking a hit to the back of his head with a spent bullet, he finds he has lost his memory:

> "'Petsamo?' Gregory murmured vaguely. "Petsamo? Where's that?"
> "Wake up, man!" Freddie laughed. "It's the Finnish port in the Arctic circle."
> A look dawned in Gregory's eyes that none of them had ever seen before; a frightened, hunted look. "But, but–" he stammered, "the Arctic! What am I doing up in the Arctic?"
> They all stood there in silence for a moment regarding him anxiously until, in a very small voice, Erika said suddenly: "You do know me, darling, don't you?"
> "Of course I do," he laughed uneasily. "As though I could forget your lovely face in a million years! But wait a minute – that's very queer – I can't remember your name."
> "I'm Erika," she said softly.

"Erika," he repeated. "That's a pretty name, isn't it – and marvellously suitable..."'[6]

And just as In *You Only Live Twice*, amnesia has a very unusual effect on his sex life, as Erika laments:

'In those hectic days they had spent in Munich and Berlin together early in November they had been the most passionate lovers. When they had met again in Helsinki his absence from her had seemed only to have increased his eagerness; but their opportunities for love-making had been lamentably few. Then his injury at Petsamo had changed his mentality in that respect as in all others. On waking on their first morning in the trapper's house he had accepted quite naturally that he was in love with her, but it had been an entirely different kind of love. He was tender and thoughtful for her and followed her every movement with almost dog-like devotion, but he did not seem to know even the first steps in physical love-making any more.'[7]

This is soon remedied, and Sallust regains his memory and completes his mission. It is likely that Fleming had read this novel: Wheatley was an acquaintance, and also a friend and close colleague of his brother Peter, who modelled the protagonist of his novel *The Sixth Column* on him. Wheatley was also one of Britain's best-selling thriller-writers, and Fleming was a thriller aficionado. In addition, both the central plot premise of *From Russia, With Love* and many of the biographical details of James Bond in *You Only Live Twice* were influenced by another Wheatley novel, *Come Into My Parlour*.

IN *FAKED PASSPORTS*, as in *You Only Live Twice*, the device of a secret agent contracting amnesia is more of an intriguing incident than a driving engine of the plot. Not so in *Pray Silence* by Manning Coles, published in October 1940, just six months after *Faked Passports*.

Coles was the pseudonym of two writers, Adelaide Manning and Cyril Coles. Their first novel, *Drink to Yesterday*, was published in March 1940 to great success (the jacket of the 1947 edition proclaimed it 'The thriller that made Manning Coles famous in a day'). *Drink To Yesterday* is set in the First World War, and ends with British secret agent Tommy Hambledon being hit on the head and shoved into the sea while undercover as a German. His colleagues in London presume he has drowned. *Pray Silence* reveals he did not, but was washed ashore, discovered, and nursed back to health. Unfortunately, he has also forgotten who he is. He is presumed to be German, and presumes so himself. As 'Klaus Lehmann', he rises to become Deputy Chief of Police in Berlin until in 1933, gazing into the flames of the Reichstag fire, he suddenly remembers his true identity and resolves to get back in touch with London and defeat the Nazis:

> "'I am Hambledon, an agent of British Intelligence. Bill, where is Bill?
> There was a crash and a roar of flame as one of the floors fell in, and Hambledon looked up. That was the Reichstag burning. "Good God," he thought, "and now I am a member of the Reichstag. It's enough to make anybody feel faint, it is indeed."'[8]

Despite its quaintness and implausibility, *Pray Silence* is a beautifully constructed, witty and thoughtful spy thriller, and a real masterpiece of the genre. It led to twenty-four sequels. Tommy Hambledon doesn't have a sex life to speak of, so we're not told of the effect of his amnesia on it, but it seems clear that Fleming also read this novel, and combined the details of both it and *Faked Passports* to come up with a new twist on the idea. Amnesia is a staple plot device of thrillers, and it has taken many forms: doctors with amnesia, murderers with amnesia, and so on. But this is much more direct. *You Only Live Twice* has four very precise correspondences with *Faked Passports*. In both novels,

1. A British secret agent
2. is struck on the head
3. and recovers to find he has amnesia,
4. with the unusual side-effect that he has also forgotten how to have sex.

There are not many novels one could say all four of these about. But *You Only Live Twice* also has six precise correspondences with *Pray Silence*. In both:

1. A British secret agent
2. on a mission under cover as a foreigner
3. plunges into the sea.
4. He survives but has amnesia,
5. and comes to believes he is his cover identity,
6. while he is presumed dead by his colleagues back home.

Taken together, there are *eight* correspondences between *You Only Live Twice* and these two novels:

1. A British secret agent
2. on a mission under cover as a foreigner
3. is struck on the head
4. and plunges into the sea.
5. He survives but has amnesia,
6. which has the side-effect that he also forgets how to have sex.
7. He comes to believe he is his cover identity,

8. and is presumed dead by his colleagues.

So many correspondences seem very unlikely to be coincidence, especially as Ian Fleming was both a connoisseur of thrillers and, as a journalist and former intelligence officer, something of a magpie. In his book on Operation Mincemeat, Ben Macintyre quotes a document written in September 1939 that, although signed by the Director of Naval Intelligence, Admiral John Godfrey, 'bore the hallmarks' of having been written by Fleming, who was his personal assistant. The 'Trout Memo' was circulated to other wartime intelligence chiefs, and was a list of ideas for deceiving the Germans. Number 28 on the list was headed 'A Suggestion (not a very nice one)':

> 'The following suggestion is used in a book by Basil Thomson: a corpse dressed as an airman, with despatches in his pockets, could be dropped on the coast, supposedly from a parachute that had failed. I understand there is no difficulty in obtaining corpses at the Naval Hospital, but, of course, it would have to be a fresh one.'[9]

Fleming was also interested in the fictional potential of amnesia: it featured in two of his other novels. The villain of *Casino Royale* was a displaced person at the end of the Second World War who feigned amnesia until being transferred to Strasbourg and adopting the name 'Le Chiffre'. And in *Moonraker*, renowned British industrialist Hugo Drax is revealed to be the villainous Graf Hugo von der Drache, a former Nazi commando who in the latter stages of the war is captured while wearing a British uniform. Like Le Chiffre, he also pretends to have amnesia and is nursed back to health as a missing British soldier by the name of Hugo Drax. This is somewhat similar to *Pray Silence*: Hambledon is the hero and genuinely has amnesia, but he is also nursed back to health by his enemies after being mistaken for one of them, and rebuilds his new life under a false identity he has adopted.

Pray Silence AND *Faked Passports* were published just six months apart, and even in the fast-moving publishing schedule of the war it seems unlikely that they influenced each other. It is more likely that some earlier source triggered the thought in the minds of Dennis Wheatley and 'Manning Coles' that led to both their novels featuring British secret agents losing their memory: perhaps an earlier novel (although I haven't found any), or a news item about a soldier returning from war with amnesia, or something similar. In *Pray Silence*, the idea has a pleasing neatness to it: what if a secret agent were under cover on a mission, somehow lost their memory, and ended up believing that they were their cover identity? In *Faked Passports*, the idea is a strangely ineffective digression that misses the idea's potential: Gregory Sallust is not under cover and so does not believe he is anyone else.

WE MAY NEVER know where the idea originally sprung from, but the ripples of it can be traced from 1940 onwards. It seems likely that Ian Fleming read both these novels and refashioned the concept into a new mixture to his own taste, featuring James Bond in Japan. Some sixteen years later, the chain continued with Robert Ludlum presenting a fresh twist on the idea. It has taken on several more forms since, from the film *The Long Kiss Goodnight* to the graphic novel series *XIII*.

The idea, with some tweaking, was also resurrected in the 2012 Bond film *Skyfall*. Taking its cue from *You Only Live Twice*, Bond is shot and plunges into water. He is presumed dead, his obituary written. We see him in a beach hut with a woman and, as in *You Only Live Twice*, he 'looks blankly out to sea with the glazed eyes of a sleepwalker'. However, there is no amnesia. *The Guardian* noted several antecedents for the film's theme of resurrection:

> 'Bond's watery plunge harkens back, of course, to the granddaddy of such feints – Holmes's plunge from the Reichenbach Falls in Arthur Conan Doyle's story *The Final Problem*, a death prompted by Doyle's weariness with his own creation...
> Maybe it was inevitable that as film franchises mushroomed... resurrection would pass up the food chain from TV soaps to high-end Hollywood movies, following the example Lt Ellen Ripley in the Alien films, who perished in a vat of molten lead at the end of *Alien 3* only to be cloned from surviving flesh tissue for *Alien: Resurrection* in 1997.
> The conceit still groaned with the memories of a hundred horror sequels – from *Halloween* to *Friday the 13th*. The movie that gave resurrection its current respectability was released just a few years later: Doug Liman's *The Bourne Identity* in 2002.
> In that film, you'll remember, Jason Bourne is shot in the back and plunges, like Bond, into another of those watery graves that never seem to last..'[10]

But of course, as we have seen, Bond's watery grave preceded Bourne's. The story has come full circle, and the influence of Ian Fleming's novels – and the vintage British thrillers that influenced them – continue to live on in surprising ways.

Notes for this chapter:

1. 'Quantum of Solace: Bourne-Again Bond' by Richard Corliss, *TIME*, November 13, 2008.
2. *The Bourne Identity* by Robert Ludlum (Granada, 1980), p61.
3. *You Only Live Twice* by Ian Fleming (Pan, 1966), pp181-182.
4. 'James at 30' by Robert Ludlum, *Entertainment Weekly*, Issue no. 123 June 19, 1992.
5. *The Man With The Golden Gun* by Ian Fleming (Pan, 1967), p21.
6. *Faked Passports* by Dennis Wheatley (Arrow, 1966), pp249-250.
7. Ibid., p404.
8. *Pray Silence* by Manning Coles (Hodder & Stoughton, 1953), p40.
9. *Operation Mincemeat* by Ben Macintyre (Bloomsbury, 2010), p7.
10. 'James Bond's resurrection: how coming back to life became a film favourite' by Tom Shone, *The Guardian*, October 18 2012.

Rogue Royale

The Lost Bond Film by the 'Shakespeare of Hollywood'

JEREMY DUNS

For Johanna, with love

AUTHOR'S NOTE

In this short e-book I look at some early attempts to film Ian Fleming's first novel, *Casino Royale*, and in particular the surviving material by screenwriter Ben Hecht. Some of this research featured in an article I wrote for the *Sunday Telegraph* in March 2011 and two articles I published on my website in August 2010, but the majority of what you're about to read is previously unpublished. I hope you enjoy it.

Jeremy Duns
Mariehamn, Åland, September 2013

Rogue Royale

IN 2006, AUDIENCES AROUND the world flocked to see Daniel Craig play James Bond for the first time, in an adaptation of Ian Fleming's first novel, *Casino Royale*. The film was a commercial and critical triumph, but it wasn't the first attempt to adapt the novel – in fact, it was the third, and the book had had a rocky journey at the hands of screenwriters and producers over several decades.

Fleming had started writing the story in January 1952, by his own account to counter his 'hysterical alarm at getting married at the age of forty-three'[1]. He wrote the book at his holiday home in Jamaica, inspired by some of his own experiences and memories of the Second World War. The resulting short novel was a heady brew of espionage, gambling and betrayal in northern France that deftly merged the traditions of vintage British thrillers with the more brutal style of hardboiled American writers such as Dashiell

Hammett. Published in 1953, it was well-reviewed in Britain, but failed to become a bestseller. Fleming nevertheless had high hopes that James Bond would become a success, either through his books or through screen adaptations of them.

He didn't have to wait too long for the latter to appear. The first adaptation of *Casino Royale* was a one-hour play performed live on American television in October 1954: Barry Nelson starred as crew-cut American secret agent Jimmy 'Card Sense' Bond, on a mission to defeat the villainous Le Chiffre, played by Peter Lorre, in a high-stakes baccarat game. Due to the format, this was a much-simplified and stagey version of Fleming's novel, with little of its extravagance or excitement. The book features a wince-inducing scene in which Le Chiffre, desperate to discover where Bond has hidden a cheque for 40 million francs that he needs to save his life, ties Bond naked to a cane chair with a cut out seat and proceeds to torture him by thrashing his testicles with a carpet-beater. This clearly couldn't be shown on television in 1954, so instead Bond was shown being placed fully clothed in a bathtub and viewers watched him howl with pain as, off-screen, Le Chiffre's men attacked his toenails with pliers.

Other changes included transforming the character of Felix Leiter, an American agent in the novel, into Clarence Leiter, a horsey British agent who at times seems more sophisticated than Bond. The novel's characters of Vesper Lynd and René Mathis were combined to form Valerie Mathis, a French agent, and the major plot twist of the novel, that Vesper is a traitor, was dropped.

To Fleming's disappointment, CBS's adaptation of *Casino Royale* came and went with little fanfare: however, other plans to film the novel were already afoot. A week before

CBS had bought the television rights to *Casino Royale*, Gregory Ratoff bought a six-month film option on the novel, and in 1955 he bought the rights outright.

An extravagant bear of a man who had fled Russia at the time of the Bolshevik Revolution, Ratoff was a well-known actor, producer and director – he had directed Ingrid Bergman's first Hollywood film, *Intermezzo*, in 1939. He was also a close friend and confidant of two of Hollywood's most powerful men, Darryl F. Zanuck of Twentieth Century-Fox, and Charles K. Feldman, the playboy super-agent of Famous Artists who represented Marilyn Monroe, Gary Cooper, Richard Burton and Lauren Bacall. Feldman was also a producer, and had already had huge success with *A Streetcar Named Desire* and *The Seven Year Itch*.

Shortly after buying the rights to *Casino Royale*, Ratoff set off on a tour of Europe, ostensibly to seek out locations. 'In fact, he was gambling,' says Lorenzo Semple Jr.[2] Now a well-established scriptwriter, having co-written *Papillon*, *The Parallax View*, *Three Days of the Condor* and, most relevantly, *Never Say Never Again*, Semple was then an unknown in his early twenties: Ratoff had scooped him up as a promising new talent and invited him along for the trip.

'Charlie Feldman and Darryl Zanuck were helping Gregory out by sending him money, as they did for years,' Semple says. 'He was a friend and someone they liked playing poker with, and Gregory knew where all the bodies were buried. But it all had to be above board – had to be for work. So there had to be a script we were working on.'

Semple says he was essentially acting as Ratoff's 'slave' – a term he uses without rancour – working on a variety of scripts for him as well as performing errands and writing letters on his behalf. Semple says that although Ratoff was genuinely interested in filming *Casino Royale*, he also used it as a pretext to travel around Europe, ostensibly researching locations but mainly gambling with funds from Feldman.

'We were going around everywhere,' Semple says, 'Paris, Lisbon, Estoril.' Ratoff was an eccentric master. In Estoril, he discovered that *Intermezzo* was playing and he and Semple went to see it. In the middle of the showing, Ratoff suddenly leaped out of his seat and pointed at one of the actors, shouting out that he was dead. 'Everyone thought he was crazy,' says Semple, 'some crazy guy in the audience.'

But when he wasn't gambling or interrupting film screenings, Ratoff was thinking about *Casino Royale*. One wild idea he mentioned was to have Bond played by Susan Hayward, but Semple says 'that was just Gregory talking'[3]. He was also putting decidedly more serious wheels in motion. In January 1956, the *New York Times* reported that Ratoff had formed an independent production company, Maribar, which he had set up in partnership with Michael Garrison, an actor-turned-agent who would go on to create the TV series *The Wild Wild West*. The article mentioned that Maribar was working on two projects: an adaptation of Sylvia Regan's 1953 play *The Fifth Season*, which Ratoff had directed on Broadway, and *Casino Royale*:

> 'The company also has acquired rights to "Casino Royale", a novel by Ian Fleming, and the plan is to film it in CinemaScope and color this summer in England, Estoril in Spain and San Remo. Twentieth Century-Fox is slated to release this feature, too.
>
> Although the author has written an adaptation, Mr Ratoff, who is now in Paris, is negotiating with a "noted scenarist, as well as with two well-known stars to play the leads," Mr Garrison said. "Casino Royale", he explained, "may be described as a World War II spy

story, set partially in the gambling casino of the title and dealing with a search for stolen Government secrets which take the principals through such colorful places as Estoril and San Remo.'"[4]

It seems that, notions of gender-swapping 007 notwithstanding, 10 months after he had bought the rights to *Casino Royale* Ratoff was still serious enough about filming it to be announcing the project in the *New York Times*, and had even secured an agreement from Twentieth-Century Fox to release it. He also appears to have been negotiating with well-known actors and a scriptwriter, and had decided where he was going to shoot the film. He knew the Italian port of San Remo well, having filmed *Operation X*, starring Edward G Robinson, there in 1950. Estoril is in Portugal, not Spain, and is a very interesting location to have chosen, as Ian Fleming's visit there in May 1941 had been an inspiration for the novel. Fleming mentioned this incident many times – here he is discussing it with his editor William Plomer in an interview from 1962:

> 'Well, the gambling scene in my first book is more or less a blown up version of what happened to me during the war, because I was flying to Washington with my chief, the Director of Naval Intelligence, and we came down at Lisbon and were told that if we wanted to go and meet some German secret agents, they were always gambling in the Casino at Estoril in the evening. So we went along and my chief didn't understand the game of *chemin de fer* they were playing. I explained it to him and then it crossed my mind to have a bash at the Germans who were sitting around, and see if I couldn't reduce their secret service funds. Unfortunately, I sat down and after three bancos my travel money had completely disappeared. Now that, greatly exaggerated, was the

kernel of James Bond's great gamble against Le Chiffre in which he took Le Chiffre to the cleaners.'[5]

The *New York Times*' article mentioned England as another filming location and the Second World War for the setting, so it may be Ratoff was considering cleaving the story more closely to Fleming's own wartime experiences instead of making a modern-day version, or one with an American agent as its hero, as CBS had done in 1954.

But the most intriguing aspect of this brief item is the passing comment that Ratoff was negotiating with a scriptwriter even though 'the author has written an adaptation'. The idea that Ian Fleming himself wrote a film adaptation for *Casino Royale* is a highly tantalizing one. Could it be true? On the one hand, articles such as this, even when in newspapers as respected as the *New York Times*, often contain inaccuracies – the location of Estoril, for instance – and the grand plans discussed in them don't always come to fruition. On the other hand, the information about Fleming having written an adaptation was not being cited to build up the film, because Michael Garrison was quoted as saying that they were choosing *not* to use it but were instead in negotiations with a 'noted scenarist'. Garrison was promoting the idea that a well-known screenwriter would be used, so it's hard to see what would be gained from inventing the idea that the relatively-unknown Fleming had written an adaptation they wouldn't use. In context, it seems an unlikely thing to have fabricated.

In addition, Fleming had already written a film adaptation of his own work, and would do so again. In 1955, the Rank Organisation had optioned his third novel, *Moonraker*, but had failed to develop it. Frustrated by his dealings with Rank's script department, Fleming had written his own screenplay of the novel.[6] Two years later, Rank paid £12,500 for the film rights to Fleming's non-fiction book *The Diamond Smugglers*, which collected a series of articles he had written for *The Sunday Times*. According to trade publication *The Bookseller*, Rank also 'commissioned Ian Fleming to prepare the film treatment'.[7] Fleming apparently agreed to provide Rank with a 'full story outline' for a further £1,000, but declined writing 'the master scene script' or to be available in England for consultations.[8]

The rights to *The Diamond Smugglers* were later bought by producer George Willoughby. In 1965, he claimed that Fleming had written a film treatment for the book for Rank that had had very little in common with the articles he had written for *The Sunday Times*, and that, for the film he was planning, the basic story 'would be based mainly on the treatment written by Ian Fleming himself'.[9]

Neither Fleming's screenplay of *Moonraker* nor his treatment for *The Diamond Smugglers* have yet come to light. Could it be that there is also an undiscovered film adaptation of *Casino Royale* from the 50s, written by Ian Fleming? If so, what could it be like? Is it set in the 1950s, like the novel, or based on his experiences during the war? And how might it differ from the James Bond films we know and love? These questions remain unanswered – for now, at least.

DESPITE THE PROMISE of the *New York Times*' item, Ratoff doesn't seem to have made any progress on *Casino Royale* following it. Before long, he had an added complication in the form of competition – from Ian Fleming. Along with his friend Ivar Bryce, Fleming had teamed up with a young producer called Kevin McClory and they were planning on filming a newly written Bond adventure, which would eventually become *Thunderball*. In his dealings with McClory, Fleming didn't fully consider the ramifications of his having already sold the rights to his first novel to Ratoff four years earlier. Instead, he promised McClory and Bryce the right to make the first Bond feature film, based on a treatment he would write.[10]

By the summer of 1959, Fleming and McClory were feeling confident enough to give an interview about the film to the *Daily Express*. Fleming had a close relationship with the *Express*: it had been serializing his novels since 1956 and had been running comic strip adaptations of them since the previous year. On June 11, the paper published an article titled 'Who do *you* think fits the part of James Bond?', which featured a gentle – and fairly obviously staged – disagreement between McClory and Fleming as to who should be cast in the part:

> 'James Bond, the tough action hero who has made £30,000 for author Ian Fleming in six best-sellers, is to be brought to the screen in a British film.
> But last night author Ian Fleming was not satisfied with the star selected to play his hero: Trevor Howard. Which is likely to cause complications for producer Kevin McClory, who is keen for Howard to have the part...'[11]

This was a more intriguing way of letting it be known that the film was forthcoming than a simple announcement. McClory gave the argument for Howard, who he felt looked as though he had 'lived it up' enough to be convincing as Bond. Fleming then provided the knock-down to this:

> 'Howard is not my idea of Bond, not by a long way. It is nothing personal against him. I think he is a very fine actor. But don't you think he's a bit old to be Bond?'[12]

Howard was 43 at the time, and Fleming stated that Bond was in his early thirties, adding:

> 'I wonder how many people who follow the James Bond strip in the Daily Express would see Howard as that character. Not many, I bet.'[13]

Fleming said he felt that Peter Finch was 'nearer to it'. When it was pointed out to him that Finch was just a year younger than Howard, he reconsidered, saying:

> 'I would be happier if the part could be given to a young, unknown actor, with established stars playing the other roles.
> Otherwise I am keen on the project. The film will not be an adaptation of one of my books. I am writing an original screenplay for it.'[14]

The authorship and ownership of the resulting story would later be a matter of much more serious disagreement between Fleming and McClory, but for now they had succeeded in stoking a 'controversy' over who should play Bond in a national newspaper, and as a result readers wrote in with their own choices, some of which were printed in the paper's letters page of June 15 1959: picks included Richard Burton, Michael Craig and Richard Todd.[15]

Peter Finch, British-born but Australian, and now best known for his role as the deranged news anchorman Howard Beale in 1976's *Network*, may seem an unusual actor for Fleming to have picked, but in the '50s he was a leading man and his latest film, which had been released by Rank in Britain in January, was *Operation Amsterdam*, a thriller about commandos trying to secure a stock of diamonds during the Second World War, with a key scene featuring a spectacular bank raid.

McClory, Fleming and Bryce continued with their plans, for the time being. On June 28 1960, *The Times* published an article titled 'Big American Film Plan For England', which began:

> 'Mr. Spyros P. Skouras announced at a meeting in London yesterday that 20th Century-Fox Film Corporation, of which he is president, has decided to make almost the whole of seven films in Britain and to release 12 British films now in the course of being prepared. The cost, placed at $20m., was estimated as probably being higher than it would be if the same programme were to be carried out in Hollywood, where the corporation's normal output of films will not be reduced as a result of the work now to be done in Britain.'[16]

The article detailed some of the proposed films:

> 'Of the British films to be released by 20th Century-Fox, Casino Royal [sic], based on a novel by Mr. Ian Fleming, will have a cast including both the recent interpreters of the character of Oscar Wilde – Mr. Robert Morley and Mr. Peter Finch...'[17]

This was once again news of Ratoff's production. Ratoff, it seems, had not yet given up on making *Casino Royale*, and still had interest from Twentieth Century-Fox – enough for the president of the company to include it in its future roster and announce it to the press.

The two actors named are also interesting. To be announced to the press in this way by Skouras, it seems likely they had both committed themselves to the film – they may even have signed contracts. Finch, of course, had been Fleming's pick for James Bond the previous year. Was his involvement coincidence, or had Ratoff or Skouras read the article in the *Express*? If so, what did they make of the fact that there was another Bond film in production, and one that Fleming was promoting? Had they snatched Finch from under the rival production's noses – and had he committed to being the first film Bond? In a further ironic twist, Finch had played the lead in *The Trials of Oscar Wilde*, which had opened in cinemas the previous month. That film was made by Warwick Films, and was co-produced by Cubby Broccoli, who had yet to enter the Bond fray. Ratoff had directed his own film, *Oscar Wilde*, starring Robert Morley as the playwright, which had also been released the previous month. It is unclear whether Ratoff was considering the avuncular Morley for the part of M, Le Chiffre or another character.

The news that Twentieth Century-Fox was planning to release *Casino Royale* was also reported in the *Los Angeles Times*, on July 7 1960, mentioning Ratoff as the director and Finch as the star.[18] McClory read it and was furious. He had been told that his company had the right to make the first Bond film. He confronted Bryce, and the acrimony spiralled towards litigation.[19]

On December 14 1960 Gregory Ratoff died, and his widow subsequently sold the remainder of the rights to *Casino Royale* to his former agent, Charles K. Feldman. But within months of securing the rights Feldman was leapfrogged, when it was announced in the press in June 1961 that some new players had entered the arena:

'The remarkable James Bond thrillers are to be filmed at last.

This will be splendid news for the several millions fans – which includes President Kennedy – of Ian Fleming's blood curdlers.

They have been bought by English producer Harry Saltzman, who produced "Saturday Night and Sunday Morning", and Albert "Cubby" Broccoli.

"Actors are falling over themselves to play Bond," Saltzman says. "Cary Grant, David Niven, Trevor Howard, James Mason, all are interested. But I want to use an unknown…"'[20]

In July, the *New York Times* filled in some of the details:

'WHOLESALE LOT: In the frenetic business of acquiring properties for the movies, it is standard procedure for a company to buy a book, play or script in competition with others. But it is extremely rare for a producer to snag practically all of an author's works for filming. Such was the case the other day when the independent production team of Harry Saltzman and Albert Broccoli, in association with United Artists, bought no fewer than seven novels by Ian Fleming, British newspaper man, to be made under the Saltzman-Broccoli corporate banner of Lowndes Productions for U.A. release.'[21]

Ironically, Broccoli was a former employee of Charles Feldman, having worked as an agent at Famous Artists early in his career. Broccoli and Saltzman would soon settle on a different name for their company, Eon Productions, although Saltzman would later form his own production company called Lowndes independently of Broccoli, with which he made such films as *The IPCRESS File* and *Battle of Britain*. The article said that the first of the films would be filmed in

England and the West Indies that autumn, that it was likely to be *Dr No*, and that they were in negotiations with Wolf Mankowitz to write the script.

But in the meantime, Charles Feldman was sitting on a potential goldmine. In March 1961, *Life* magazine had listed *From Russia, With Love* as one of John F. Kennedy's 10 favourite books, and sales of the Bond novels were now soaring in the United States. At some point in 1962, Feldman approached Howard Hawks to direct *Casino Royale*, and the two met with screenwriter Leigh Brackett to discuss it. Hawks liked the idea of Cary Grant as Bond, but after seeing a print of *Dr No*, which premiered in London that October, he dropped out of the project.[22]

Unbowed, Feldman commissioned Ben Hecht to write a script. Known as 'the Shakespeare of Hollywood', Hecht was an acclaimed novelist, poet and playwright. He had worked on several classic screenplays, including *The Front Page*, based on the play he co-wrote, and had been nominated for six Oscars and won twice, for *Underworld* at the first Oscars ceremony in 1927 and for *The Scoundrel* in 1935. With *Underworld* and *Scarface*, he created the template of the modern gangster film, and he also had a fruitful collaboration with Alfred Hitchcock, writing *Spellbound* and *Notorious*, as well as working uncredited on dozens of other classic screenplays, including *Gone With The Wind* and *Foreign Correspondent*.

Feldman had worked with Hecht before: in 1954, he had commissioned him to ghost-write the memoirs of his client Marilyn Monroe, although Hecht's resulting work would not be published for another 20 years. Hecht had also worked for Feldman uncredited on the scripts for *Walk on the Wild Side* and *The 7th Dawn*.

Hecht's papers are stored in the Newberry Library in Chicago. According to Alison Hinderliter of the library's Manuscripts and Archives section, the collection arrived in 'total chaos' in 1979 as the result of the death of Hecht's widow, which resulted in the urgent need to gather everything from her apartment in New York before it was thrown out. Much of the sorting of the 94 cubic feet of material was done by a single volunteer in 1981.

The Newberry houses over 3,000 folders of material relating to Hecht's prodigious output, including drafts, correspondence and other material related to over 70 screenplays, many of which are classics, so it's perhaps unsurprising that the contents of Box 3, Folders 131-136, 'Casino Royale, 1967', have never received any critical analysis or attention from outside the library. But these papers shed light on an extraordinary lost chapter of cinema history, and feature some of the most surprising and exciting adaptation of Ian Fleming's work, written by one of the greatest screenwriters of the 20th century.

THE NEWBERRY'S *CASINO ROYALE* folder contains over 500 pages of material, including six screenplays, at least five of which are by Hecht. An early screenplay dated April 20 1957 with no name on the title page may be a vestige of Ratoff's European excursions, and is a faithful adaptation of the novel in several ways but for one crucial element: James Bond isn't in it. Instead of the suave but ruthless British agent, the hero is Lucky Fortunato, a rich, wisecracking American gangster who owns a string of casinos and is an expert poker player.[23] Semple says he didn't write it, but there were others Ratoff might have called on, including his assistant George St

George. Some of Charles Feldman's papers are stored at the Louis B Mayer Library in Los Angeles, but they were unable to yield a date or further context for the following note from Feldman to Hecht:

> 'Dear Ben,
> Please call me after you have read the enclosed script and attached notes. My telephone number at the house is CRestview 5-2339. Am sure I'll be there. Best,
> Charlie.'[24]

It may be that the 1957 draft is this 'enclosed script' Feldman sent Hecht, perhaps as a starting point to see what he could do with it. With Hecht's expertise in gangster films, he would have been a natural choice.

Of the remaining material, two of Hecht's drafts are undated and the rest are from various points in 1964. There are also hand-written notes, correspondence (one letter mentions it has enclosed two cheques for his work, valued at $2,000 each[25]) and some notes for an outline dated December 17 1963 – just two months after the premiere of the second Bond film, *From Russia With Love*, in London. The last dated pages are from April 14 1964, so it looks like for at least four months Hecht worked on adapting Ian Fleming's first novel.

For Hecht, this was a remarkably long time. He was an infamously fast writer, often working around the clock; he wrote *Nothing Sacred* in two weeks and finished the script of *Scarface* in just nine days. But *Casino Royale* was a problematic novel to adapt for film. On the one hand, it is one of Fleming's strongest novels (Raymond Chandler and Kingsley Amis both felt it his best): intense, almost feverishly so, and rich in characterization and atmosphere. But it is also very short – practically a novella – with little physical action other than the torture scene. Bond falls in love with his fellow agent on the mission, Vesper Lynd, and even considers proposing marriage to her before he discovers that she has been coerced into working for SMERSH and has betrayed him, leading to his being tortured. Vesper kills herself, and the novel ends with Bond savagely reporting to London that 'the bitch is dead now'.

Hecht was approaching the novel 10 years after it had been published, but these aspects of the book still presented a challenge. His December 1963 outline notes appear to be his first attempt at coming to grips with the novel, and particularly the problem of its brevity. Across eight pages, he sketched out a prelude to the novel's plot that would serve as a first act and bring the running time up to scratch.

The set-up he outlined is that M sends Bond on a mission to find Gloria Dunn, a beautiful young singer and the daughter of England's leading nuclear scientist, who has gone missing. Hecht had clearly read Fleming's *Thunderball* – published in 1961 and soon to lead to legal action from Kevin McClory – as the main villain here is not SMERSH operative Le Chiffre, but 'Number 1', the head of international crime syndicate 'Specter', an Americanised spelling of that novel's SPECTRE. Number 1 has built a sex- and drug-trafficking empire using 5 million rubles he has been given by Soviet intelligence, and he now invites a Russian intelligence officer, Tautz, to join Specter and help them all become richer. His plan is to sell Moscow highly classified intelligence, which he will obtain by extorting senior figures around the world: Gloria Dunn has been kidnapped and fed drugs until she has become an addict, and the threat of her becoming a prostitute will force her father to work for them. The action moves from Baghdad to Algiers to Naples, and culminates in a raid on a German castle that Specter is using as a brothel: Gloria and her father are both tortured and killed, and Hecht ends the notes with the phrase: 'Here begins the Casino Royale plot'.[26]

These pages contain plenty of intriguing ideas, but as a whole the plot isn't an exciting one: several elements of it feel hackneyed, and apart from Bond and M none of the characters from the novel feature, making the fact that it has been tacked on all the more obvious.

Hecht soon abandoned the missing daughter plot, which feels a little too run-of-the-mill for a Bond film – though it's interesting to note how similar it is to recent films such as *Spartan* and *Taken* – but developed another strand from these pages much further. Fleming's novel opens with Le Chiffre already in trouble: he has embezzled SMERSH funds to run a string of brothels in France but has lost huge sums as the result of a new law that has closed many of them down. Now he is desperately hoping to win his money back at baccarat before SMERSH discover it is missing and kill him. Bond, the British Secret Service's finest gambler, is sent to the casino in France to make sure he loses.

Le Chiffre's brothel-keeping establishes that he is villainous, and seedily so, but we never see him in that line of business in the novel. Hecht made vice central to his plot, with Colonel Chiffre, as he becomes, actively controlling a network of brothels in which he secretly films powerful figures in order to extort secrets out of them for Specter.[27] So just as the theme of Fleming's *Goldfinger* is avarice and power, the theme of Hecht's *Casino Royale* is sex and sin. It's an idea that seems obvious in hindsight, and Hecht used it both to raise the stakes of Fleming's plot and to deepen the story's emotional resonance.

This is visible in the surviving pages of two separate but overlapping drafts. Neither has a date attached, but judging from some of the scenes both were written after the December 1963 notes but before drafts from February and April 1964. Among the few surviving letters about *Casino Royale* in Hecht's papers is one he wrote to Feldman on January 13 1964 in which he says he has 110 pages of 'our blissful Casino Royale' ready to be typed and sent, but that if Feldman can wait three days he will have finished the finale, resulting in 130 pages of what he refers to as a first draft. As there is no other material dating from January 1964 in the folders, it seems likely that these excerpts are from then. Hecht also added that he had 'never had more fun writing a movie'.[28]

Both drafts feature a British secret agent called James Bond, who gambles against a Colonel Chiffre, alias Herr Zero (there are no references to 'Number 1' here or in any subsequent drafts), is aided by an American agent called Felix Leiter and a French agent called René Mathis, and falls in love with Vesper Lynd. Both drafts stick very closely to the atmosphere of the novel, while adding several new plot elements and characters. These include one of Chiffre's former brothel madams and a former lover of Bond's: at different points she is named Mila Brant, Mila Vigne and Giovanna Scotti, but in all guises she is a classic *femme fatale*, trying to seduce Bond by breaking into his bedroom:

> 'Bond becomes alert in the shadows. He listens intently.
> He hears a faint sound in the adjoining bedroom.
>
> Gun in hand, Bond moves cautiously to the bedroom.
> He switches on the bedroom light, and stands with his

gun aimed at the lovely occupant of his bed. It is Giovanna. She is in a transparent nightie.

> BOND
> (politely)
> Good evening, Giovanna.
>
> GIOVANNA
> You are not surprised?
>
> BOND
> No.

He starts undressing.

> How much did you pay the concierge to get in?
>
> GIOVANNA
> Twenty francs. A bargain. May I have a cigarette?
>
> BOND
> (handing her one)
> Here. Don't set the bed on fire.
>
> GIOVANNA
> I do not need a cigarette for that.'[29]

The dry cynical wit and unashamed sexual appetite are more in keeping with Sean Connery's version of Bond than Ian Fleming's, although both elements had already become synonymous with the character, and have remained so. For James Bond, the natural response to finding a semi-clothed beautiful woman in his bed is to start undressing himself, and a subsequent stage direction has him continuing to do so 'as calmly as if he were alone in the bedroom'. Giovanna notes his lack of hesitation:

'GIOVANNA

(smoking)
You remind me of my first lover. No kissing. No hugging. Boom! – his clothes off and into bed.

She pats his naked belly.

Darling, you're adorable.

BOND
In what way?

GIOVANNA
You know I am employed by Colonel Chiffre. And you say nothing.

BOND
It would only spoil an interesting night for both of us.'[30]

Hecht pulled off a very neat trick here: the dialogue sounds as though it must have featured in a Bond film before, and yet is wholly original. That's hard enough to do for any writer, but Hecht was tailoring his story to fit a formula that was being established as he wrote. Elsewhere, he has Bond wine and dine in much the same way as in the novel – he even creates a new cocktail, mixing Black Velvet for Vesper in a crystal pitcher with Champagne, Bass Ale and rye whiskey as they eat caviar.[31] But the tone here is unmistakably that of the cinematic Bond, recalling some of the more overtly sexual moments in the early films, such as this exchange in *From Russia With Love*:

'TATIANA
I think my mouth is too big.

BOND
I think it's a very lovely mouth. It's just the right size – for me anyway!'

Hecht takes the innuendo just so far, and then withdraws. Bond's banter with Giovanna is suddenly interrupted by Vesper telephoning the room, claiming she has been poisoned. Bond leaves at once, disappointing Giovanna. 'Be brave,' he tells her as he closes the door.

ANOTHER NEW CHARACTER in these drafts is Dr Mesker, who is also working for Chiffre. However, he is a much weaker addition than the playful Giovanna. He can read minds, and scratches his cheek and taps his nose while watching the baccarat to signal to Chiffre which cards his opponents have. When Felix Leiter implausibly figures out what is happening, Bond responds in the next round of the game by thinking of different cards when he looks at his own, so that Mesker transmits the wrong signals to Chiffre, who then starts to lose. This is absurd and rather hammy, though it leads to an effective scene in which Chiffre accuses Mesker of betraying him, and Mesker reads Chiffre's mind and realizes that his own death is imminent at the hands of a brutal henchman:

> 'MESKER
> Never! I did not! No, no! I never betrayed you. Don't! Colonel Chiffre, don't say it! Don't say it! Oh, God, don't speak it – no!
>
> CHIFFRE
> (quietly)
> Erik. Finish.'[32]

Hecht may have been inspired here by Fleming's second novel, *Live And Let Die*, in which the villainous Mr Big is aided by a fortune-teller, Solitaire, but it's hard to imagine film audiences accepting the idea in this form. There is no ambiguity about Mesker's telepathic powers — it's no trick but a real supernatural gift — and Bond accepts the possibility too readily to be convincing.

Much more effective is a scene that directly follows, in which Chiffre is informed that Bond and Vesper have been spotted on the beach at Royale. One of his henchmen, Black Patch — the novel's character, given more to do — suggests killing Bond with a telescopic rifle:

'CHIFFRE
No shooting. Bullets inspire police inquiries. Inquiries might interfere with my Casino play tonight and tomorrow. I have no more time than that. The death of Bond must seem an accident.

BLACK PATCH
(smiling)
The boat?

CHIFFRE
Yes. Bond will go swimming.'[33]

This is followed by Black Patch and another henchman, Anton, attacking Bond's boat on water-skis. Anton places a bomb on board, but Bond kills him by skewering him with a boat hook and leaps into the water before the explosion, later to be picked up by René Mathis and the French coastal patrol.[34]

These two undated drafts share a lot of similar material, but only one continues to the end of the narrative: Bond returns to London following Vesper's death, where M tells him to take a holiday in Jamaica. Bond says he would rather stick around in case M has any errands for him, clearing the way for his next mission.[35] Perhaps Feldman planned to slot *Casino Royale* into the existing EON series, as he didn't have the rights to any other Bond novels — or perhaps he felt there was a possibility of creating sequels of original Bond stories using his existing rights.

THE 47 SURVIVING PAGES of the draft dated February 20 1964 elaborate on many of the scenes and ideas from earlier pages, with varying degrees of success. The draft opens with a pre-titles sequence — itself a nod to the ongoing films — in which Felix Leiter arrests senior United Nations diplomats and several beautiful prostitutes who have ensnared them in honey traps.

This is followed by the most unusual sequence in all of Hecht's material, and his boldest departure from both the source material and the film series. On the surface it's the traditional briefing scene between M and Bond, complete with a prelude of Bond flirting with Miss Moneypenny, but for one change — he is no longer James Bond. Instead, he is an unnamed American agent who M gives the name James Bond. M explains that 'since Bond's death' MI6 has put several agents into operation using his name: 'It not only perpetuates his memory, but confuses the opposition.'[36] He adds that Bond, as he will henceforth be known by everyone, will have to change his tailor, haberdasher and gun to fit in with his new identity.

The new Bond comments that he won't drink martinis but will stick to his bourbons, and there is some discussion of his having previously owned a casino in Jamaica. But after this scene the character is referred to as Bond both in the script and by all the other characters, and is in every way indistinguishable from Bond. It's a very odd addition, but there may have been pragmatic reasons for it: Feldman could have decided to make the film with someone other than Sean Connery as Bond, and instructed Hecht to add a short scene to explain it. Perhaps he had an actor in mind, as the obvious strategy would have been for M to give the operation to another British agent rather than an American one.

M briefs his new Bond on Specter's extortion operation in the United Nations and elsewhere, and sends him to Hamburg to work with fellow MI6 agent Vesper Lynd to investigate one of Chiffre's palatial brothels. Bond isn't keen on the idea of a woman being involved in such a mission:

> 'BOND
> I should think a female on this job would be sort of coals to Newcastle.
>
> M
> Not Miss Lynd. Extremely upright, honorable and moral.
>
> BOND
> Sounds like quite a novelty.
>
> M
> Her father Jonathan Lynd was an 0-0-7 man. Killed in our service two years ago. Vesper has been in training to take his place. Fine linguist, and her target score for last year was ninety five, point four.'[37]

Hecht introduced some new characters in this draft. One of them is cleverly extrapolated from Fleming's novel: in Chapter Two of the book, there is a passing reference to an MI6 agent who has infiltrated Le Chiffre's set-up as one of his mistresses, 'a Eurasian (No 1860) controlled by Station F'. From this, Hecht created Lili Wing, a beautiful but drug-addicted Eurasian madam working for Chiffre. Like the earlier Mila/Giovanna character, she has previously had a fling with Bond, but she is bisexual and is now doted on by her girlfriend Georgie, who carries a black kitten on her shoulder.

This draft has a notably dark, adult sense of humour. The theme of vice corrupting virtue is writ large: Vesper is poised, graceful but initially priggish, while Bond is an unrepentant lady-killer who makes fun of her innocence – until he falls in love with her. Some of the sexual references are politically incorrect even for the 60s – even for a Bond film in the 60s – with politicians attracted to children and a car chase through Hamburg's red light district concluding with a sequence in which Bond escapes his pursuers by diving into an arena where two women are mud-wrestling. He accidentally tears the wig off one, and eventually manages to escape in a blizzard of confusion and laughter from the crowd:

> 'His body covered with mud, the bewigged Bond rises out of the ooze…'[38]

It's Roger Moore's Bond a decade in advance, with some added kinkiness. It doesn't really work.

THE DRAFT PETERS out, with several of the latter pages paraphrasing passages from the novel, and the final scenes are missing altogether. The most significant – and successful – addition is the character of Gita: Chiffre's wife. She returned in the final surviving drafts, which are dated April 8, 10 and 14 1964. The April 8 section is 85 pages, and covers most of the plot: a handwritten scrawl above the date on the first page marks it as 'Incomplete Script'. The April 10 screenplay is 157 pages long and is a complete script, from 'FADE IN' to

'FADE OUT' – the title page also has a handwritten note by Hecht saying 'Copy of the draft sent to Feldman 4/10/64'. The April 14 material is 49 pages long and is marked 'Rewrite': this contain variations of many scenes from the drafts of April 8 and 10, as well as additions and improvements to earlier material. Combined, these drafts give us Hecht's final and complete screenplay of *Casino Royale*.[39]

Much of the material is familiar from earlier drafts, but gaps are filled in and it's now noticeably more assured and coherent. The dialogue crackles throughout. Bond has several bone-dry one-liners, and one can easily imagine Connery's style and delivery when reading them. In one scene, he drives around hairpin bends overlooking the Mediterranean at four o'clock in the morning, and Vesper notices a car in pursuit. Bond wants to slow down to let her jump out, but she insists on staying to help and crawls over the top of her seat into the back of the car:

'VESPER
(as she does)
I'll shoot at their tires.

BOND
No. At their heads, if you don't mind.'[40]

In two lines, Hecht punctures a cinematic cliché and nails James Bond's laconic but ruthless humour. There are many such satisfying moments, particularly in the interplay between Bond and Vesper. She feels Bond is rash and sexist, while he sees her as a school-marmish irritant. It's very recognizably the relationship of the novel, as well as of a thousand mismatched cop films since, but Hecht makes it sing. The 2006 adaptation had a few scenes along these lines, with Vesper's initial meeting with Bond on the train being perhaps the highlight. That flirtatious needling dynamic suffuses the April '64 pages. When Vesper gives Bond twenty million francs from M, she asks him to turn away as she takes it from a money belt beneath her dress. 'It's going to be quite a strain working with you,' Bond notes wearily.[41]

The first third of the story follows Bond and Vesper as they track down thousands of rolls of film incriminating leading politicians that Chiffre has collected for Specter, which are being transported from a warehouse in Hamburg by guarded van (Specter itself is, as SMERSH is in the novel, a largely unseen threat). Vesper infiltrates Lili Wing's brothel as one of the escorts, and Bond pretends to be one of her customers while they are being filmed, but with no sound, trying to prise information from her while feigning a seduction.

The Hamburg chase – the mud-wrestling scene remains – culminates in Lili Wing being captured by Chiffre's men and fed into the crusher of a rubbish truck, while Bond uses Chiffre's beautiful wife Gita as a shield. She is shot by Chiffre's men by mistake. Bond manages to commandeer the van by impersonating one of the henchmen in the darkness, but during a subsequent car chase across the Swiss Alps the van goes over a cliff and explodes with the film rolls in it, Bond naturally escaping at the last moment.

This means Bond has wrecked the extortion operation, and Chiffre has lost half of the funds Specter has allocated to him to boot. Chiffre now needs to get the money back before Specter realize it is missing and kill him. The action relocates to the resort of Juan-les-Pins on the Côte d'Azur. Bond, in a white-jacketed tuxedo at the wheel of his Bentley, waits outside a hotel for the glamorous young Giovanna. They visit a nearby casino, where Bond coolly wins two thousand dollars at roulette, but he is then summoned to his room, where Vesper is waiting for him with instructions and twenty millions francs from M. They're to leave at once for Casino Royale, a five-hour drive down the coast, where Chiffre is determined to win back the money he lost at baccarat. The car chase ensues, they arrive at Casino Royale, and we are into the main plot of the novel.

There are many bold and ingenious ideas here. In the book, Le Chiffre and Bond duel without ever having met previously – there is also little build-up to it, as Hecht realized in his earliest outline ideas. By making Bond directly responsible for Chiffre's precarious situation, and the reason he sets up the baccarat game in the first place, Hecht uses the main body of the novel as a second act rematch between the two men. In addition, Chiffre's wife has been facially disfigured as a result of Bond's actions, so she and her husband are doubly hell-bent on vengeance.

The character of Gita Chiffre served another purpose for Hecht, who felt that the novel's extended torture sequence was seriously flawed. In a handwritten letter, unaddressed but most likely to Feldman, and undated but from context probably written after the release of *From Russia With Love* in October 1963, he explained that he felt that Le Chiffre's monologues while he tortured Bond in the novel were 'fatally inept', 'cheap' and 'comical', and that to feature one man torturing another while naked in any film adaptation would seem not only to be indulging in 'a far-fetched and unmotivated type of cruelty', but that Bond himself would come across as a 'yelping pansy'.[42]

The language is distasteful, but these were the times Hecht was working in, and he was being paid to write a film that would appeal to a mass audience – anything that didn't serve that aim would have to be changed. Like many supremely talented people, Hecht could be arrogant and scathing about flaws he perceived in others' work: 'Even Saltzman has known better than to let such Fleming pitter patter seep into his two movies,' he wrote in the same letter.[43] Hecht knew Harry Saltzman, as he had worked on a 1956 Bob Hope-Katharine Hepburn film Saltzman had produced, *The Iron Petticoat* – Hecht had become so incensed by Hope's gag writers reworking his script that he had insisted his name be removed from the credits, and had even placed an advert at his own cost in *The Hollywood Reporter* denouncing Hope.[44]

The second and third acts of the April '64 pages are broadly faithful to the novel. In a closely followed game of baccarat, Bond beats Chiffre and cleans him out to the tune of 80 million francs, with Chiffre taking 'loud slow sniffs' from his inhaler as the tension rises. The mind-reader Mesker is still present, but there is no subsequent scene in which he is killed while foreseeing his own death, which leaves the possibility for undiscovered deception rather than supernatural gifts. As it becomes clear Bond is winning, Chiffre's henchman Otto approaches Bond's chair and sticks a cane in his spine, announcing it's a silent gun and Bond will seem to have fainted if he doesn't withdraw his bet by the count of ten. The tension mounts as he counts quietly in Bond's ears, before Bond heaves back and smashes down on the cane with the crossbar of the chair, breaking it in half. The crowd is shocked as Bond goes sprawling across the floor, but he is soon back at the table and the game resumes. This is all almost identical to the corresponding scene in the novel.

Bond wins, leaving Chiffre slumped at the table to collect his winnings, then Vesper is seemingly kidnapped from the casino and he pursues her. He is waylaid by iron spikes thrown on the road, only to be captured by Chiffre, who wants Bond's cheque to save him from Specter's wrath. Now we have Hecht's version of the torture sequence – and it is a virtuoso piece of writing. Bond is stripped naked and tied to a chair with the seat cut out, as in the book, but now Chiffre is accompanied by his wife, who we see for the first time since she was shot as a result of Bond's actions: part of her jaw is missing, so that the right side of her face 'hangs unhumanly boneless', and she speaks metallically through a tube inserted into her ripped out larynx:

> 'GITA
> You remember me, Mr. Bond?
>
> BOND
> (coolly, as he stares up)
> You're a bit changed.
>
> GITA
> You will be changed, too, Mr. Bond.'[45]

Chiffre demands that Bond tell him the location of his winning cheque, while goading his wife into thrashing him with a special weapon:

> 'It is a thin, four-feet-long wooden rod. On its end is a thin slab of wood, six inches square. The implement looks like a cross between an oversized fly-swatter and undersized rug beater.
> Gita's misshapen face grimaces at the implement in her hand. She is possibly smiling.'

Gita strikes Bond repeatedly, but Bond still refuses to reveal where he has hidden the cheque. At one point Chiffre tells his raging wife to stop hitting Bond for a moment, adding, in a line a hundred European character actors would surely have sold their grandmothers to deliver: 'M'sieur Bond may want to change his mind while he is still a m'sieur.'[46]

Bond still refuses to break and, when asked about the cheque again, manages to force out a reply through the pain: 'Up your gizzard, you fat pimp.'[47]

Chiffre also waterboards Bond with whisky in an attempt to get him to talk, forcing his mouth open with the barrel of a gun while he pours the liquid down his throat. The whole scene is watched by two Doberman Pinschers, who howl excitedly along with Bond. It's an electrifyingly sinister scene.

Just as it seems that Bond is destined to die, he is rescued by masked Specter agents, who scar his hand so they will be able to identify him in any future operations, rather as happens in the novel. The agents then shoot Chiffre, who has hidden in a cupboard. The 'brothel Napoleon', as Bond calls him, dies fittingly, with silk dresses and négligées draping his blood-soaked corpse.

Bond recovers, but is rendered impotent, and Vesper visits him in his clinic, all much as in the novel. After Vesper acts suspiciously over a mysterious phone call, Bond accuses her of lying to him, but when she becomes hysterical Bond apologises, explaining he is 'a bit of an amateur about love'[48]:

'VESPER
(softly)
Don't hate me.

BOND
You're quite mad.

   He holds her in silence for a moment. Then –

Will you marry me, Vesper?

VESPER

(whispering)
Marry you?

BOND
Yes. I think we ought to legalize our quarrels. Care to answer me, now?

VESPER
Yes! Yes! I'll marry you! For as long as you want.

BOND
Good.

VESPER
(clinging)
Only – don't look at me with 007's eyes.

BOND
(grinning)
I guarantee the bridegroom will wear a grooming look.
I'll dig up a parson tomorrow – in London.

They stand locked in an embrace.'[49]

But, as in the book, it all goes wrong. The next morning, Bond waits in the lobby of the Royale with suitcases packed, ready to fly back to London, but Vesper isn't answering the phone in her room. Perturbed, he runs up the stairs and enters: Vesper is lying, undressed, on the bed. Bond thinks she is ill, but she tells him she has written him a letter explaining everything, and he sees that her eyes are cloudy:

'BOND
What have you taken?

VESPER
Cyanide. You can't help. It's almost over. Painless and efficient.

> BOND
> Why?

> VESPER
> I think you know.

Bond is silent.

> You've known, but you refused to believe. That I'm a fraud. A double agent. For M – and for Specter. That telephone call last night – Specter insisting I continue my activities – for them. I've been very remiss, for some weeks.

Bond sits in silence and stares at her.

> I was going to be married a year ago. My fiancé worked for M. he was captured by Specter. Death sentence. I pleaded for him. They made a deal with me. They'd let him live and hold him as a hostage for three years, if I worked for them. I agreed. Because he was young, and I thought I loved him very much.

Her voice has lowered.

> Can you hear me darling?

> BOND
> Yes. Plainly.

> VESPER
> It was easy at first. They were after Chiffre – same as you. It was like working together – with you.

> BOND
> You kept Specter informed of my movements.

> VESPER
> Yes.'[50]

Unlike in the novel, Vesper didn't stage her kidnapping, as she was working for Specter, not Chiffre, but she knows Bond can never believe her or trust her again, so she has taken her own life. Bond tells her he believes her anyway, and the scene ends with her dying, Bond sitting motionless beside her.

Also unlike the novel, there is no payoff of Bond calling M in London and uttering the infamous line 'The bitch is dead now'. Instead, a grief-stricken Bond is consoled by his doctor, who prescribes him with testosterone. A minor character, Georgie, returns to offer her consolations, and Bond embraces her. He is delighted to find that his body responds, and order is restored as he plants two solid kisses on her mouth and we fade out.

DESPITE THIS CONVENTIONAL ending, Hecht's April 1964 draft is phenomenal, and could have made for an extraordinary Bond film. Hecht captured all the best elements of the novel and wove them into a rich, thrilling adventure. His James Bond is a blend of Fleming's character and Connery's interpretation of him, and yet – impossible to imagine before reading it – with greater depth than either.

In parts it's reminiscent of one of his most famous scripts, that for the Hitchcock classic *Notorious*. Like *Casino Royale*, *Notorious* is both a spy thriller and a love story. Cary Grant plays T.R. Devlin, a suave and ruthless secret agent who is charged with looking after Alicia (Ingrid Bergman), the 'notorious' daughter of a neo-Nazi who drinks too much. But the cynical Devlin slowly falls in love with her, and becomes increasingly desperate to protect her from the dirty espionage game he has brought her into. Hitchcock's *North by Northwest* is often cited as an influence on the Bond films, but the character of Devlin is much closer to the character of 007 than advertising executive Roger Thornhill, even if the action in the film is much more subdued. In Hecht's *Casino Royale*, the cynical agent also falls in love with the woman he initially sees as a nuisance, although Bond drinks almost as much as Alicia.

The Bond films Hecht's drafts most resemble are *From Russia With Love* and *On Her Majesty's Secret Service*. As in the former, the plot involves sex extortion, although it is not Bond who is the target here. And as in *On Her Majesty's Secret Service*, Bond falls in love and proposes, only for his woman to die – although these are also similarities in the two novels, of course. Hecht's treatment of the romance element is powerful and, even with the throwaway ending, it's perhaps darker than any existing Bond film. There are several false notes, particularly with the sexual shenanigans, but the drafts are stuffed to the brim with ideas, the vast majority of which are dazzlingly effective. Hecht managed to cram in all the excitement, glamour and dry wit one would expect from a Bond film, and several moments of fantasy, but the themes are adult, and the violence is brutal rather than cartoonish – just as in Fleming's novel. It's a master-class in thriller-writing.

BUT, OF COURSE, it was never filmed. On Thursday April 16 1964, Hecht sent a letter to Feldman saying he would write up a critique of their 'current script' on Monday. He added some comments on Bond, including that he felt the character was 'the first gentleman-Superman to hit the silver screen in a long time', as opposed to Spillane, Hammett and Chandler's 'roughneck supermen'.[51] But Monday never came: Hecht died of a heart attack at his home on Saturday April 18 while reading.

Feldman went on to try to strike a deal with Broccoli and Saltzman, asking them to loan Connery to him for *Casino Royale*. When they turned him down, Feldman offered to make the film in partnership with them. According to Broccoli, he entered negotiations with a completely untenable offer: 75 percent of the profits for him, the remainder for Broccoli, Saltzman and United Artists:

> 'I loved Charlie. We had been friends for years. But the deal he proposed was so bizarre, if he had been my agent he would have tossed the offer – and the person making it – out of the window.'[52]

Having finally managed to get his hands on a working screenplay for *Casino Royale*, it does seem bizarre that Feldman made such an offer. But perhaps the time it had taken, together with the expense, had led him to feeling he needed that sort of stake for it to have been worth it. He may also have overestimated how far he could push his former employee. The truth was that Broccoli no longer needed him – and wasn't afraid to say so.

The deal fell through. It seems that at one point Feldman even claimed that the film of *Goldfinger* plagiarized 'a key situation' from *Casino Royale*, and threatened to sue[53] – it's unclear what the basis for this claim is, although the scene in *Goldfinger* in which gangster Mr Solo is crushed at a scrap yard is somewhat reminiscent of Lili Wing's death.

Furious that he had not come to an agreement with Broccoli and Saltzman, Feldman then approached Sean Connery to see if he would be interested in jumping ship.

Connery said he would for a million dollars, but this was too much for Feldman's blood and he turned him down.[54] He decided to take a new tack, signing an unknown Northern Irish actor, Terence Cooper, who he kept on salary for two years, and recruiting Orson Welles, David Niven, Peter Sellers, Ursula Andress, Woody Allen and several others to the project, which was now to be a wacky send-up of the Bond films. A set report in *Time* in May 1966 revealed that after Hecht's 'three bashes' at the script, it had been completely rewritten by Billy Wilder, after which Joseph Heller, Terry Southern, Wolf Mankowitz, John Law and Woody Allen had all taken their turn at it. Much of the film was improvised on the spot.[55]

Very little of Hecht's material made it to the screen, and parts that did – such as the blackmail films and the idea of calling other agents James Bond – mushroomed to absurd proportions, joining a plot that featured Bond's daughter by Mata Hari being kidnapped by a flying saucer. Feldman's budget and ambitions spiraled out of control: *Time* noted that, having failed to secure Connery, he had decided to make *Casino Royale* 'the Bond movie to end all Bond movies',[56] while in an interview with *Look* Woody Allen said Feldman wanted to 'eliminate the Bond films forever'.[57]

If any film could have done that, it was this one. Eventually released in 1967, it was a bloated and incoherent comedy that wasted the prodigious talent it had assembled, and the title *Casino Royale* was linked for decades with a cinematic disaster rather than Fleming's novel. Finally, in 2004 EON gained the rights to the novel, and set about filming it with Daniel Craig soon after.

THERE ARE STILL SEVERAL intriguing gaps in the *Casino Royale* story. Who wrote the 1957 Lucky Fortunato script? Did Fleming write a script or treatment, and if so, what was in it and what happened to it? Little research has been done into some of the other scripts for this film, some of which were by world-renowned writers. But Hecht's material nevertheless fills in a missing chapter in the history of the James Bond series.

Perhaps the most significant question raised by Hecht's drafts is what would have happened if Feldman had come to an agreement with Broccoli and Saltzman, and *Casino Royale* had been made around 1965 or 1966, or if he had gone it alone and made the film much as Hecht scripted. Perhaps such a film would have flopped, with or without EON and with or without Connery, as even a disfigured villainess and water-ski chases might not have been enough for viewers so recently awestruck by Odd Job's hat and the Aston Martin DB5's ejector seat. There are very few gadgets – although in one draft Vesper saves Bond's life with a purse that has a pistol built into its side – and although Hecht's Bond is as suave, ruthless and laconic as Connery's incarnation of the character, as in the novel he falls in love, and pays the price for it, both of which would have been radical departures at this point in the series.

Then again, perhaps such a film would have been a commercial and critical success. Hecht's drafts deepen Bond as a character, but they're still breathlessly exciting. A film based on this material would have taken the series in a different direction, and if popular might have averted the superficiality and excess that afflicted many of the films after *Goldfinger*. If Hecht's *Casino Royale* had been a success, more heavyweight scriptwriters might have been tempted to write Bond films, and the series might have gained far greater critical stature, perhaps being seen more along the lines of Hitchcock's films. *Casino Royale* might have been regarded as not just a great Bond film, but as a great thriller.

The idea that a Bond film could be a great film in its own right has been unthinkable for most of the series' duration. But Hecht's scripts represent the possibility of a Bond film that combined all that was great about the early Connery films and *On Her Majesty's Secret Service*, and might even have bettered them. Writing after the 2006 version of *Casino Royale* starring Daniel Craig, the fact Hecht managed to do this doesn't seem quite as unbelievable as it would once have been. Before then, the idea of Fleming's first novel as a straight adaptation seemed fraught with problems. Would the title, tainted by the 1967 farrago, resonate with new audiences? How could one ever hope to update a taut novel set solely in a small resort in northern France for the expectations of a modern Bond film?

The 2006 film proved it could be done, and expectations of what can be done with Bond have been pushed still further in *Skyfall*. But it is nevertheless almost head-spinning to think of the possibility of Connery doing something like this in the 60s, bringing all we think of as great in his performances and, without losing any of it, managing to bring even more. That's the truly enthralling what-if of this film that never was. We'll never know, of course, but Hecht's surviving material offers a glimpse into a cinematic genius at work, and an alternate James Bond adventure as rich, compelling and visceral as anything yet brought to the screen.

FROM THE AUTHOR

Thank you for reading this book. Authors live on recommendations, so if you enjoyed it (or even if you didn't), please spare a minute or two and write a review of it and spread the word. I'd be most grateful.

Information about and links to my other books is on my website, and my Amazon pages in the UK and US. You can also find me on Twitter, Facebook and you can contact me via email at jeremyduns@yahoo.com – I'm always interested in hearing readers' thoughts, so don't hesitate to get in touch.

Thank again,

Jeremy Duns

Acknowledgements

I would like to thank the following for their generous assistance with the research of these articles.

Gold Dust
Dave Jenkins and family; Cecilia Blight and Ann Torlesse of the National English Literary Museum in Grahamstown, South Africa; Maria Morelli and Michael Lynch of Boston University; Rebecca Cape at The Lilly Library, Indiana University; John Pearson, Peter Janson-Smith; Evan Willnow; and a special thanks to Ajay Chowdhury for his great editorial guidance.

Uncut Gem
Jon Cleary; Paul Collard and the Collard family; Fergus Fleming and Sarah Fairbairn of Ian Fleming Publications; Richard Todd; Meg Poole at the Richard Stone Partnership; Professor Zachary Leader; Stephanie Thwaites at Curtis Brown; the information officers of the Mitchell Library, the State Library of New South Wales, Australia; Sue Hodson at the Huntington Library, California, United States; Jean Cannon at the Harry Ransom Center, Texas, United States; the staff of the Swedish Film Institute Library, Stockholm, Sweden; Lisa Thompson at Jonathan Clowes, Ltd, London; Peter Knight at Knight Features, London; and Laura Watson at the Writers' Guild of America, West.

Commando Bond
M.R.D. Foot and Lieutenant-Colonel Ewen Southby-Tailyour.

Black Tie Spy
Guy Hamilton; Victor Laurentius; Lynn Hodgson; Renu Barrett at McMaster University Library, Ontario; Sophie Bridges at the Churchill Archives Centre, Cambridge; and Colleen Kelley at the Special Collections of the University of Iowa Libraries.

Bourne Yesterday
Enid Schantz and Steve Coles.

Rogue Royale
Alison Hinderliter and the staff of the Newberry Library; and Ihsan Amanatullah for his perceptive advice.

Notes

[1] 'Bon Vivant and the Scourge of SMERSH: The Master of Agent 007' by Tim Green, *Life*, August 10 1962.
[2] Semple to author, January 11 2011. All subsequent quotes from Semple from same interview.
[3] Semple has told this story before – see 'Lorenzo Semple, Jr: The Screenwriter Fans Love to Hate' by Steve Swires, *Starlog*, Issue 75, October 1983, and Semple's 'Journal' article in *Slate*, November 25 1997.

[4] 'By Way of Report' by A.H. Weiler, *New York Times*, January 8 1956.
[5] 'The Writer Speaks', Ian Fleming and William Plomer in conversation, 1962 – precise date unknown, transcript courtesy the Archives and Special Collections, Durham University Library.
[6] p276, *Ian Fleming* by Andrew Lycett, Phoenix, 1996.
[7] p1808, *The Bookseller*, Compendium of Issues 2698-2714, Publishers' Association, Booksellers' Association of Great Britain and Ireland, 1957.
[8] p317, Lycett.
[9] Letter from George Willoughby to John Collard, June 21 1965, courtesy of the Collard family. For more about the long-running attempts to make a feature film of *The Diamond Smugglers*, see my article in *The Sunday Times* of March 7 2010: 'How Ian Fleming's book on gems was neglected'.
[10] p25, *The Battle for Bond* by Robert Sellers (Tomahawk Press, 2008).
[11] 'Who do *you* think fits the part of James Bond?' by John Lambert and Peter Evans, *Daily Express*, June 11 1959.
[12] Ibid.
[13] Ibid.
[14] Ibid.
[15] 'The Rush To Cast James Bond', *Daily Express*, June 15 1959.
[16] 'Big American Film Plan For England', *The Times*, June 28 1960.
[17] Ibid.
[18] 'Hamilton Leads in "Act One" Race', *Los Angeles Times*, July 7 1960.
[19] pp86-87, Sellers.
[20] 'A Rush To Be James Bond', *Sydney Morning Herald*, June 25 1961.
[21] 'Passing Picture Scene' by A.H. Weiler, *New York Times*, July 16 1961.
[22] p595, *Howard Hawks: The Grey Fox of Hollywood* by Todd McCarthy (Grove Press, 2000).
[23] April 20, 1957, Box 3, Folders 131, 131A, 131B, 131C and 131D, Ben Hecht Papers, Midwest Manuscript Collection, Newberry Library, Chicago.
[24] This message was visible via searching the Louis B Mayer Library section of the American Film Institute's website in January 2011. Unfortunately, library manager Robert Daicopoulos was unable to

find either this or any other correspondence between Feldman and Hecht in the register or archives, and the collection has been closed for several years and doesn't appear likely to reopen in the near future. Daicopoulos to author, January 1 2011; see also 'The lost Feldman files and the loss of direction at the AFI: A personal reflection on archives' by Thomas Kemper, *Film History: An International Journal*, Volume 22, Number 3, 2010, pp309-312.

[25] Letter from Famous Artist Productions to Ben Hecht, Box 57, Folder 1227, Hecht Papers. The letter is undated, but mentions that the cheques are dated February 7 and 15 1964.

[26] pp1-8, Notes for an outline on *Casino Royale*, December 17 1963, Box 3, Folder 136a, Hecht Papers.

[27] The idea of blackmailing senior figures by listening in to their conversations in a brothel may have been inspired by the Salon Kitty, a famous Berlin bordello that was taken over by German intelligence in the Second World War.

[28] Letter from Hecht to Feldman, January 13 1964, Box 67, Folder 1888, Hecht Papers.

[29] p31, undated material. Box 3, Folder 132, Hecht Papers.

[30] Ibid.

[31] Ibid., p26.

[32] p20, undated material, Box 3, Folder 133. A version of this scene is in the other undated draft (p37, Box 3, Folder 132), but there the henchman is called Otto.

[33] p39, undated material, Box 3 Folder 132.

[34] Ibid., pp40-41. In the other undated draft, Bond swims out to a raft and two henchman, here named Jago and Mitzik, approach him on water-skis via a speedboat, and one clubs Bond over the head – the pages then skip ahead so the end of the scene is missing. pp21-23, Box 3, Folder 133.

[35] pp56-57, Box 3, Folder 132.

[36] p9, February 20 1964 draft, Box 3, Folder 135.

[37] Ibid., p12.

[38] Ibid., p42.

[39] One peculiar difference between the pages is the question of Bond's identity: in the April 8 and 10 drafts he is the real Bond, while the April 14 pages revert to the counterfeit idea.

[40] p69, April 10 1964 draft.

[41] Ibid., p65.

[42] pp2-3, undated handwritten letter, Box 3, Folder 134, Hecht

Papers.

[43] Ibid. The reference to 'two movies' – if I have correctly read his handwriting – suggests this was written after *From Russia With Love's* release.

[44] 'Ill-Fated Bob Hope-Katharine Hepburn Comedy, Gone for Four Decades, Returns' by Mike Barnes, *The Hollywood Reporter*, October 25 2012.

[45] p141, April 10 1964 draft, Hecht Papers.

[46] Ibid., p145.

[47] Ibid., p146.

[48] p53, April 14 1964, draft, Box 3, Folder 136A, Hecht Papers.

[49] Ibid., p54.

[50] Ibid., pp56-57.

[51] p96, Letter from Ben Hecht to Charles K Feldman, April 16 1964, Box 3, Folder 136B, Hecht Papers.

[52] pp199-200, *When The Snow Melts* by Cubby Broccoli with Donald Zec (Boxtree, 1998).

[53] p267, *United Artists* by Tino Balio (University of Wisconsin Press, 2009).

[54] p57, *Kiss Kiss Bang Bang* by Alan Barnes and Marcus Hearn (The Overlook Press, 1998).

[55] 'On Location: Little Cleopatra', *Time*, May 6 1966.

[56] Ibid.

[57] 'Who Is the Real James Bond Anyhow?', *Look*, November 15 1966.

Made in the USA
Lexington, KY
07 June 2019